Life is a Kaleidoscope Coloring Book
By
Jason Jones

First Edition Published by Faith by Grace Publishing

First Faith by Grace Publishing Printing 2016.

ISBN-13: 978-0692652923

ISBN-10: 069265922

A record of the Library of Congress serial number can be acquired from the publisher.

Manufactured in the United States of America

Cover and Layout by Ashlea Ingram

Images drawn by Jason Jones

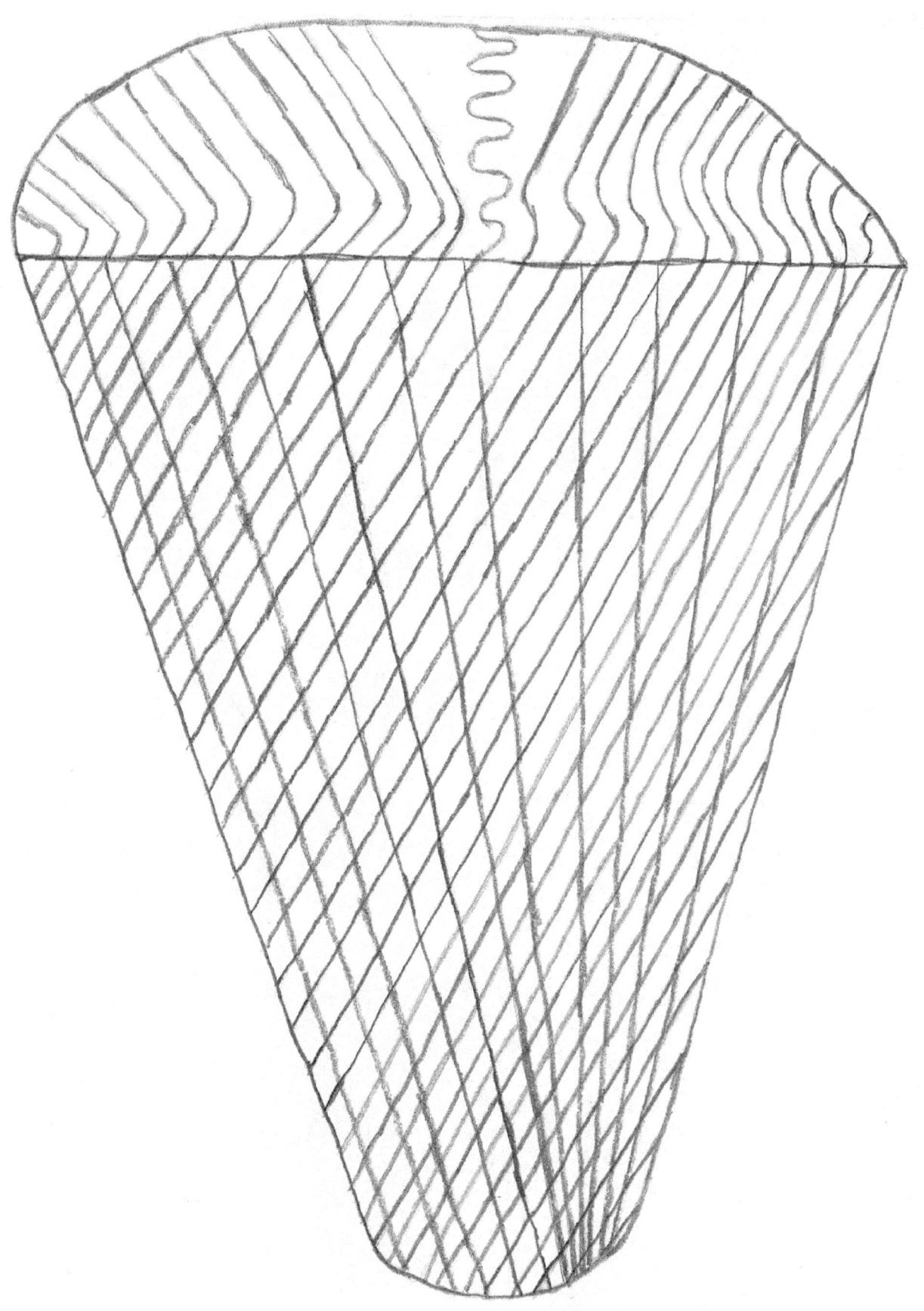

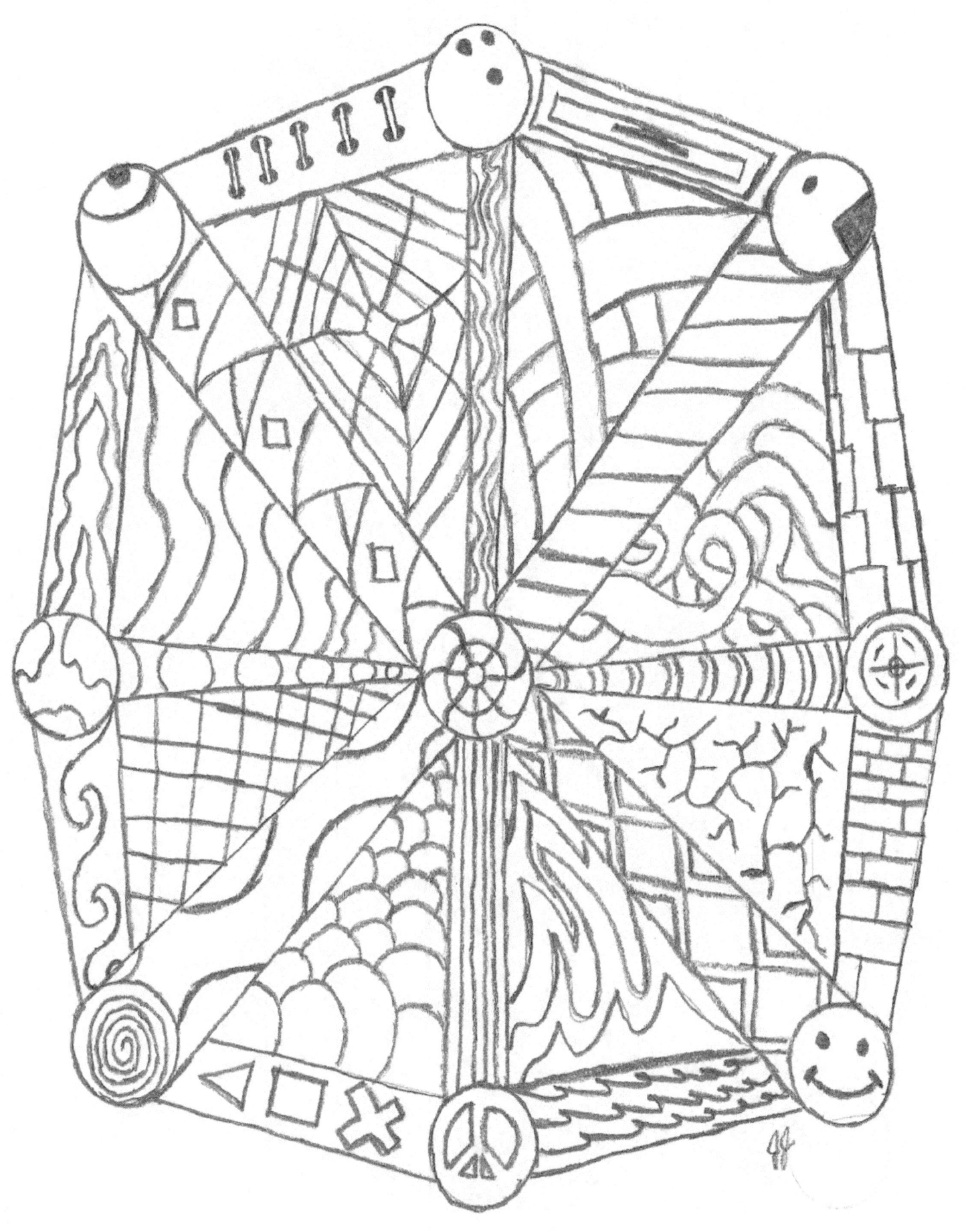

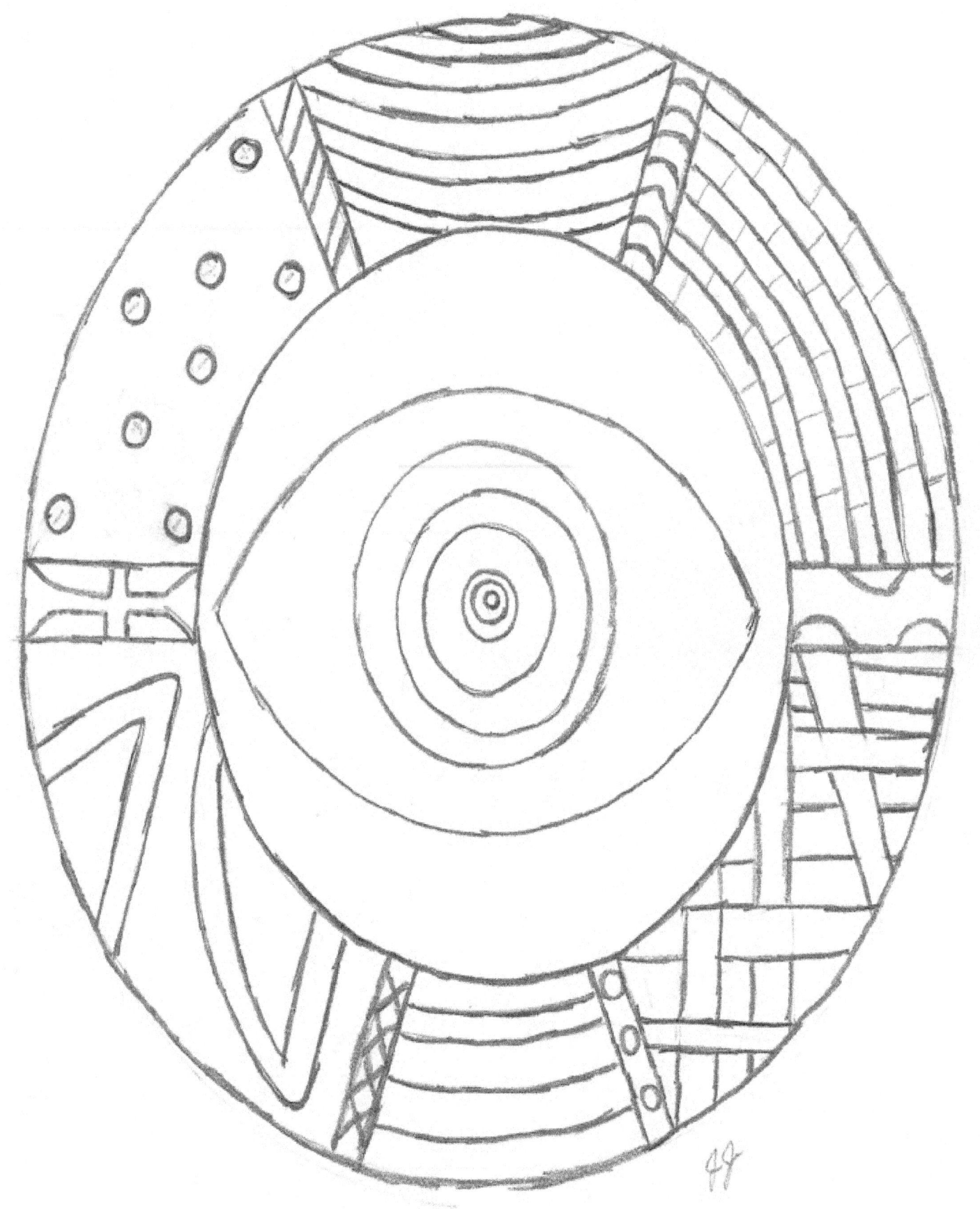

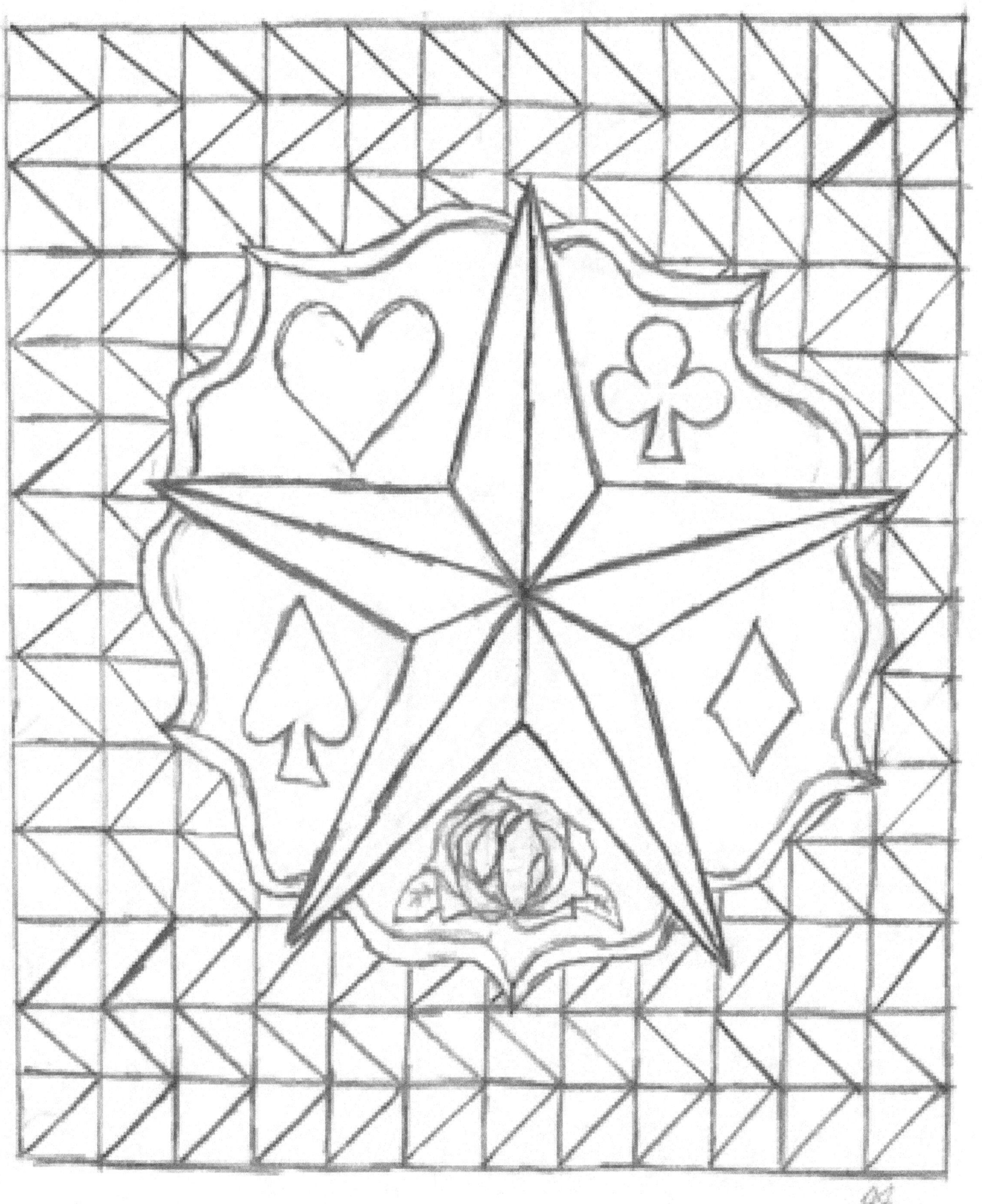

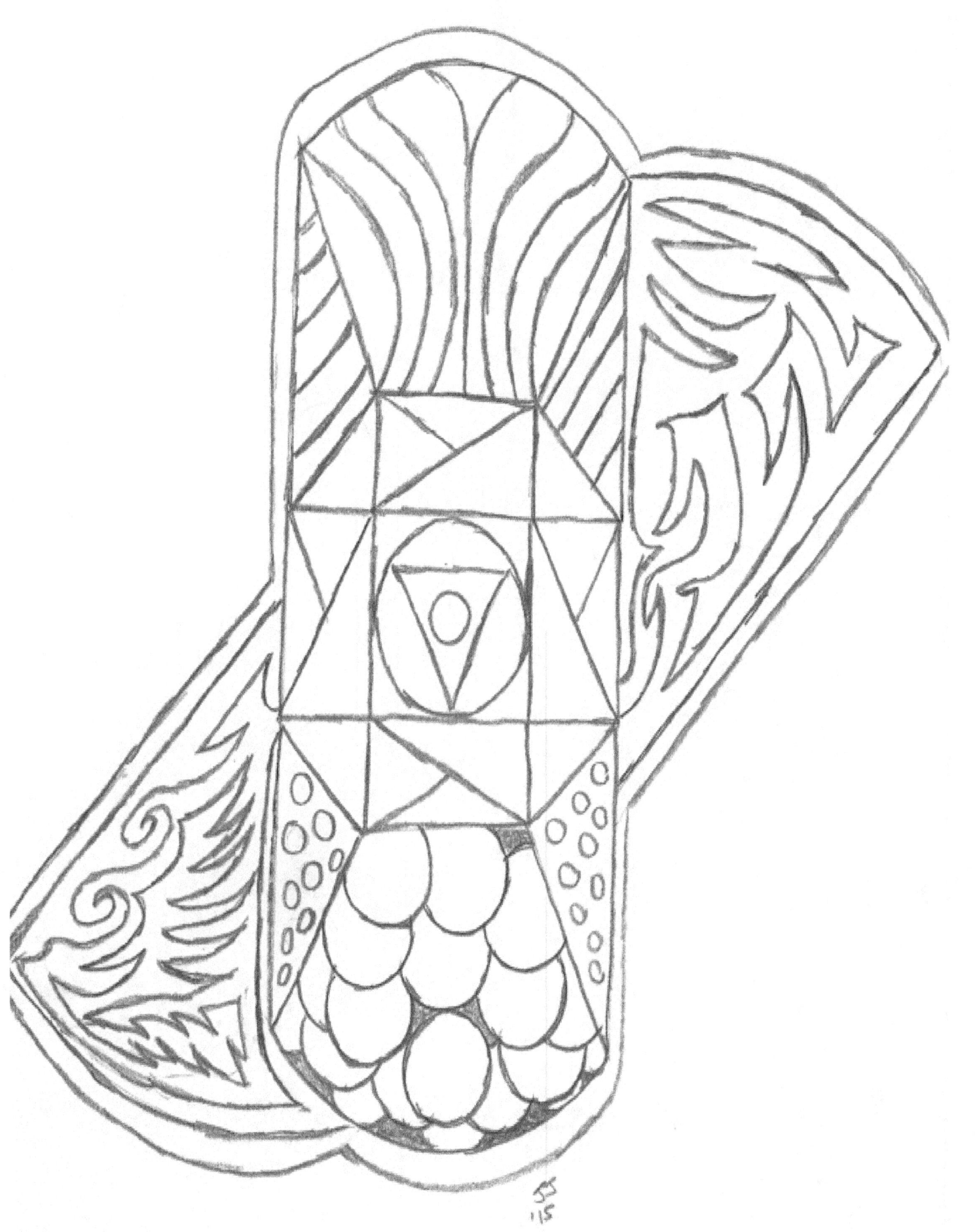

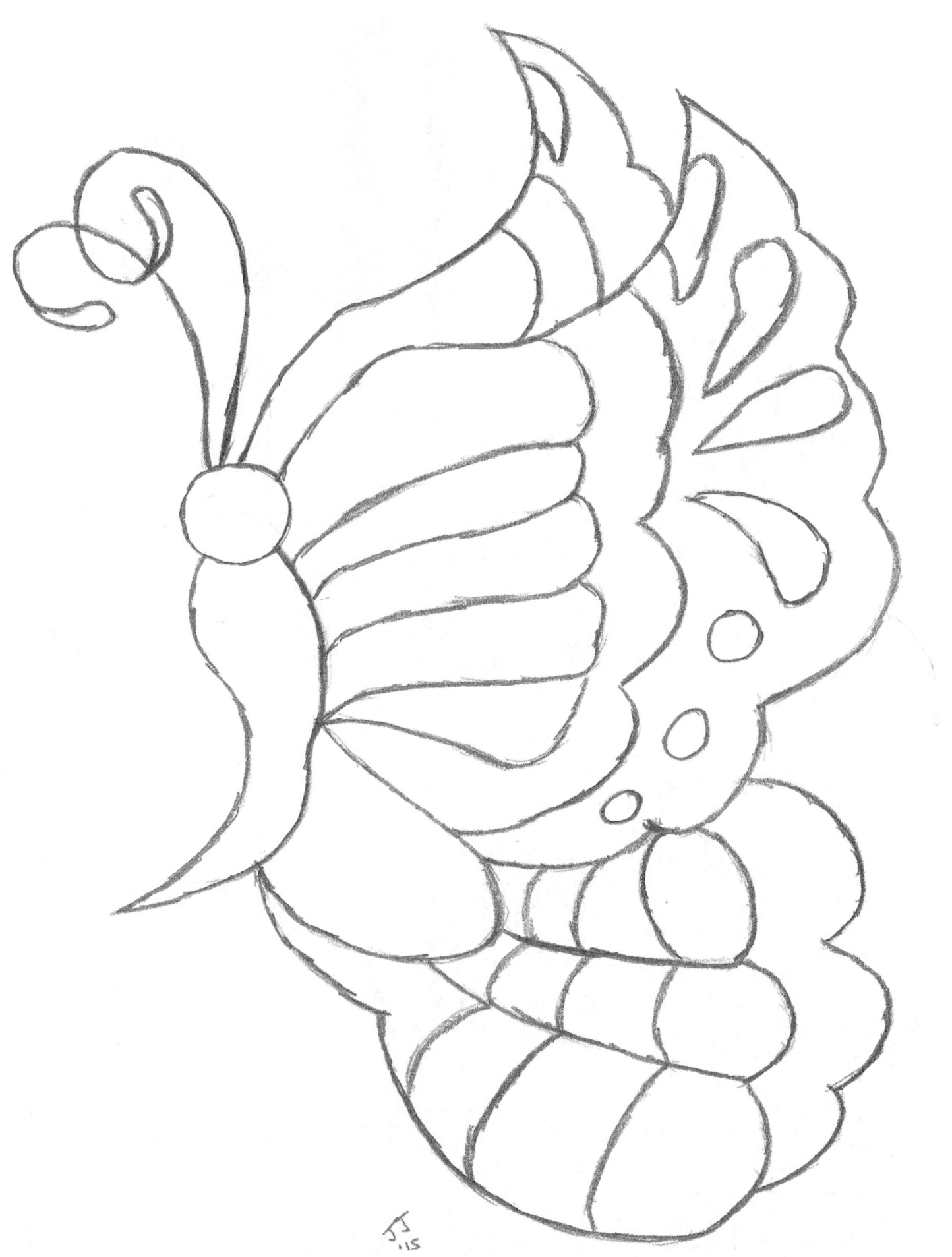

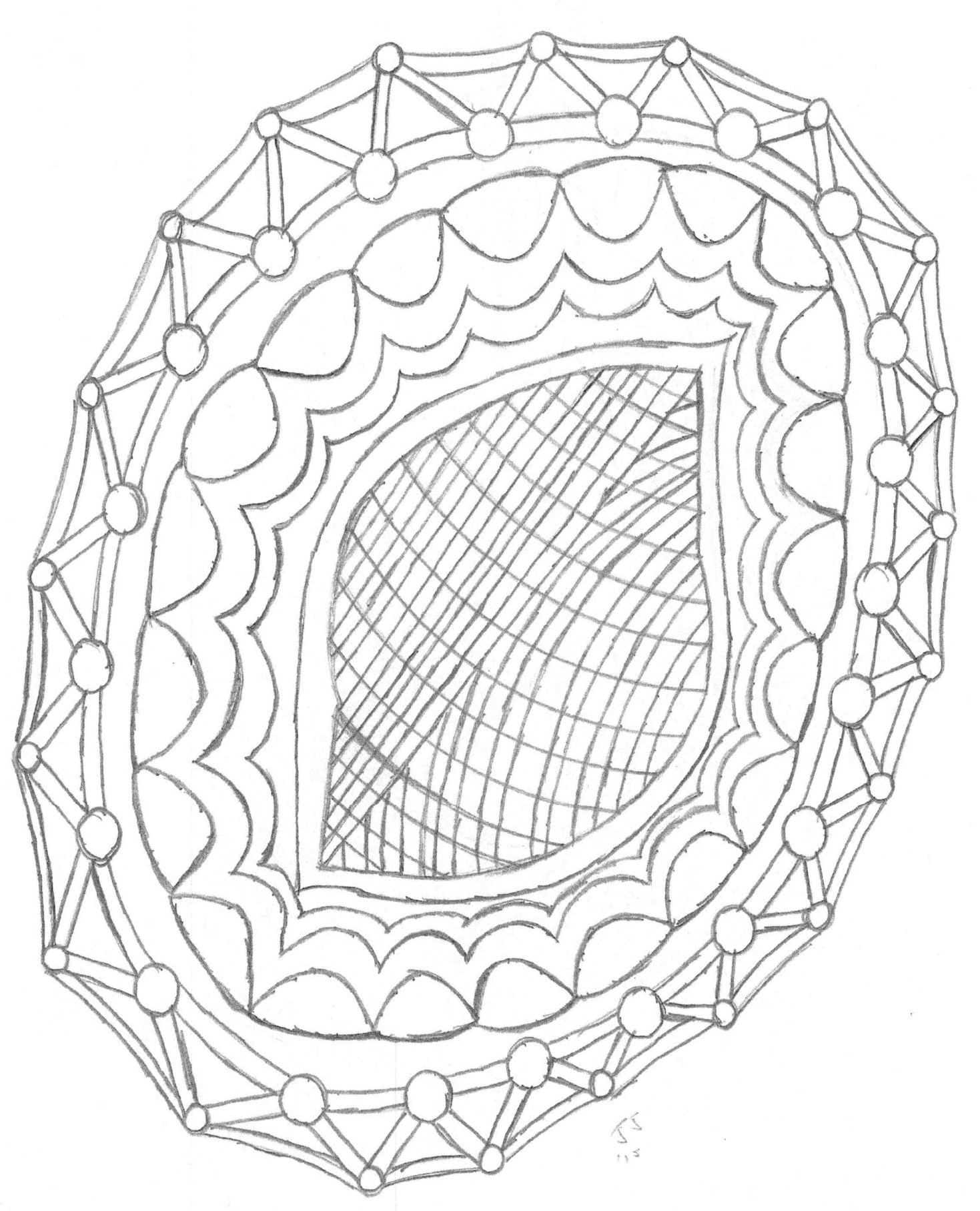

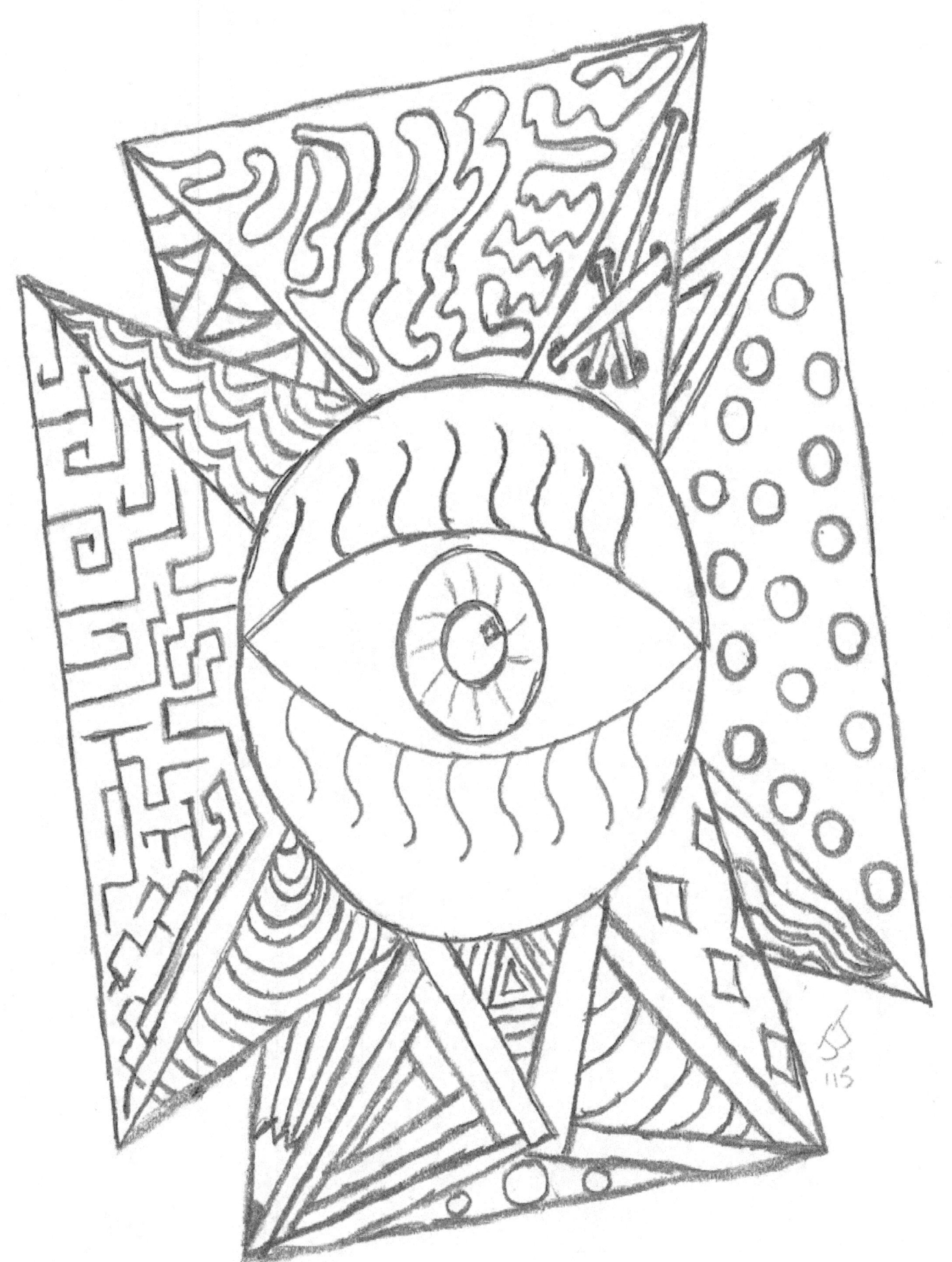

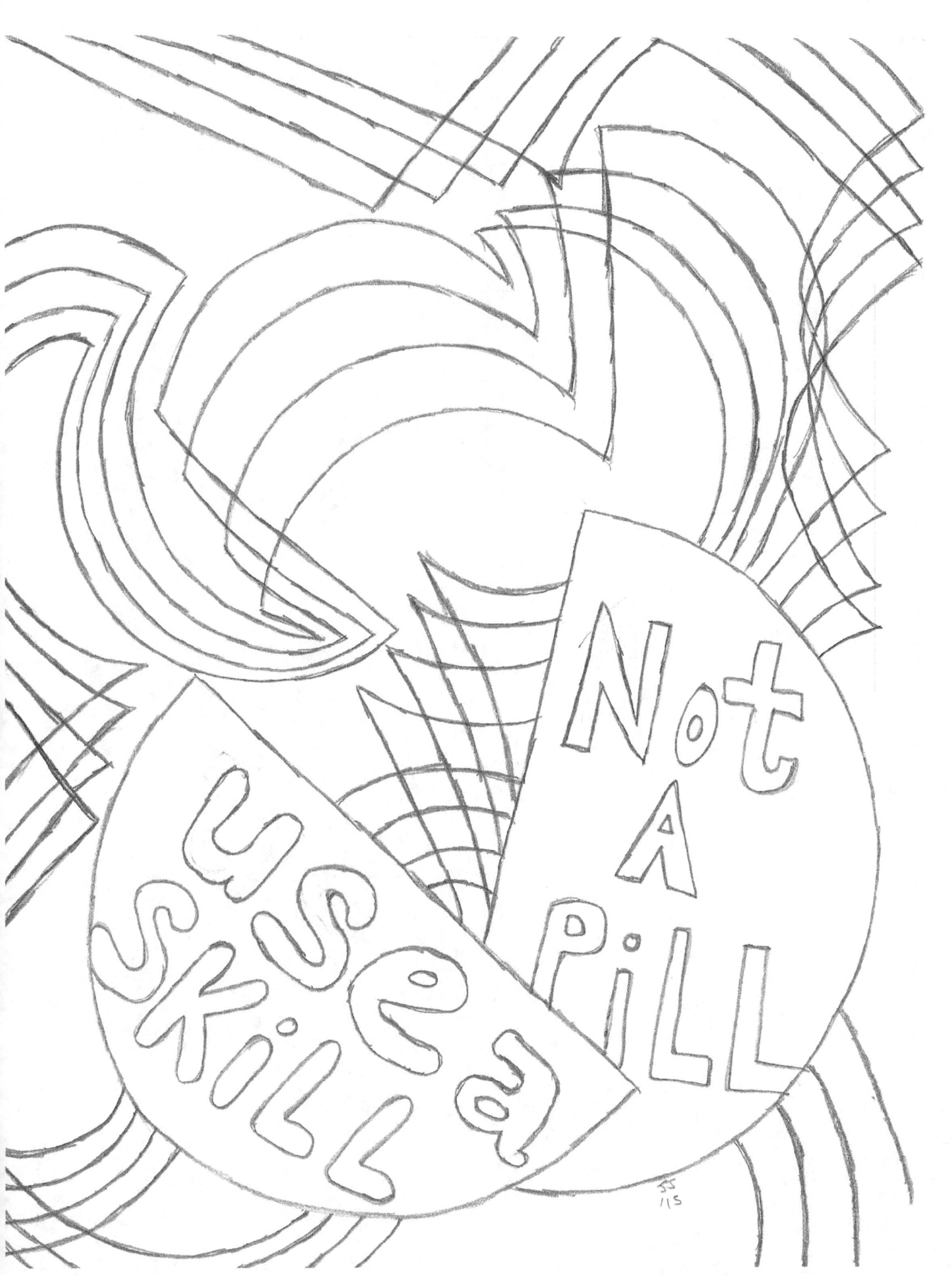

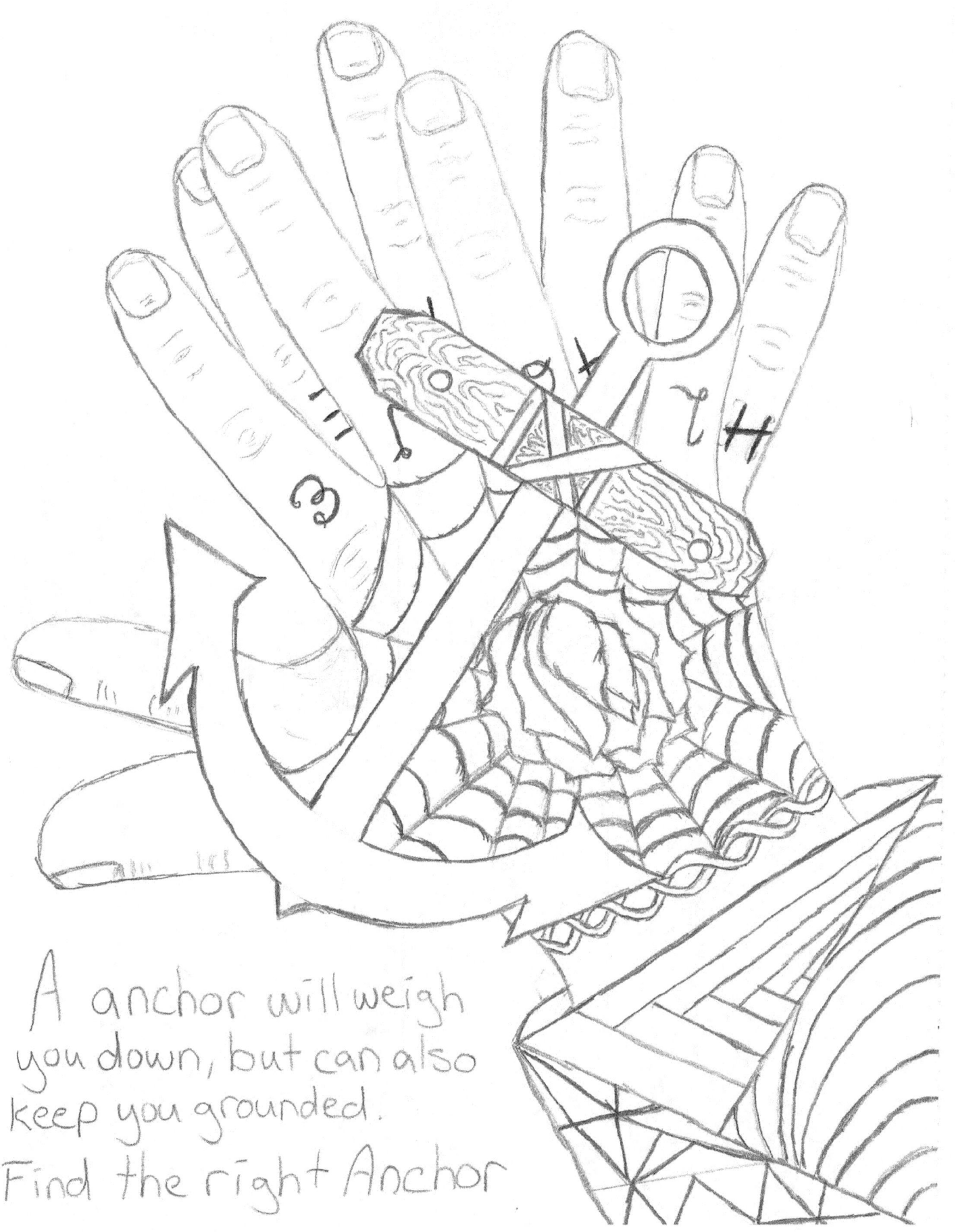

A anchor will weigh
you down, but can also
keep you grounded.
Find the right Anchor

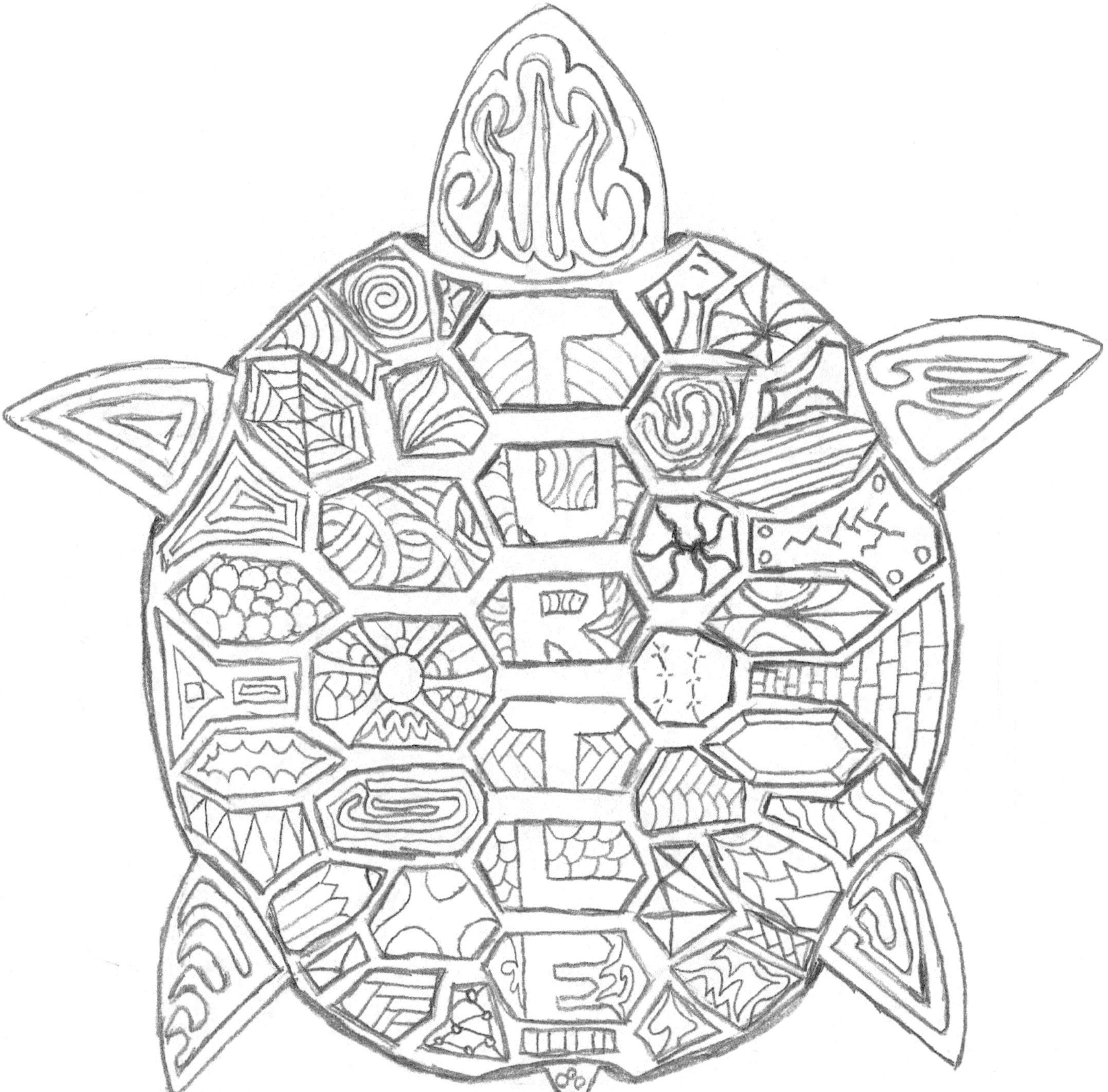

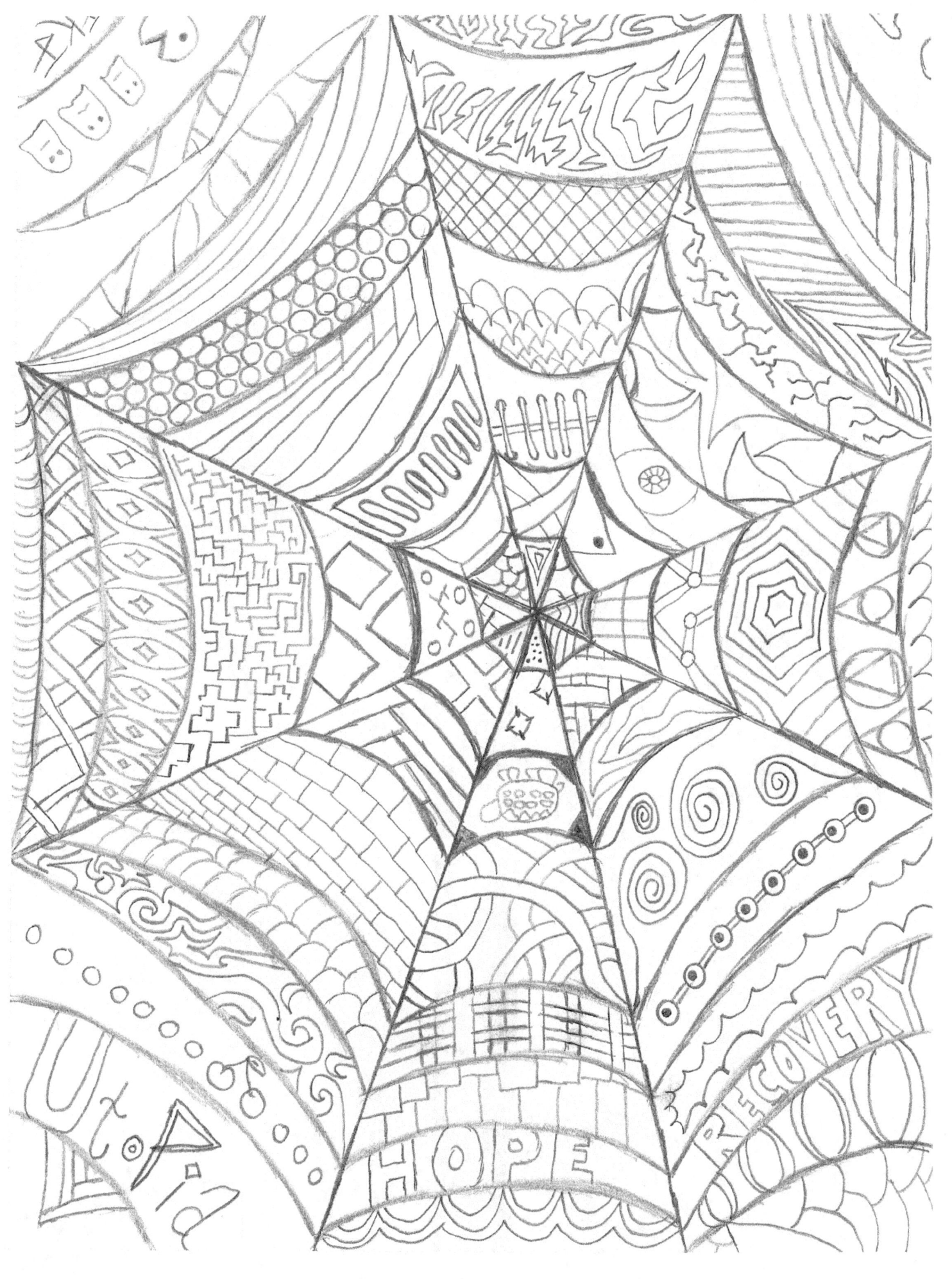

Post
Traumatic
Stress
Disorder

You can't
patch a wounded
Soul with a band-aid

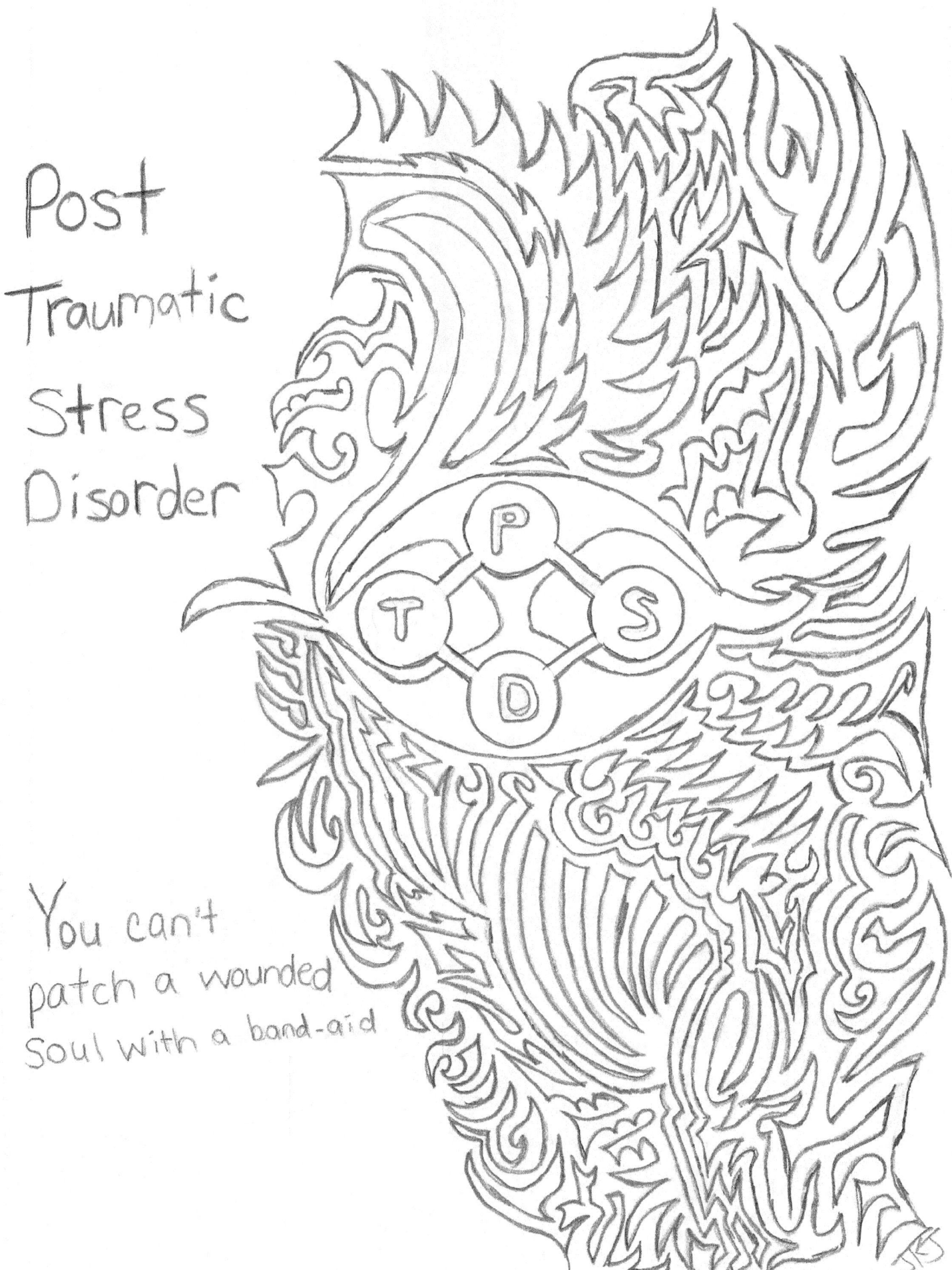

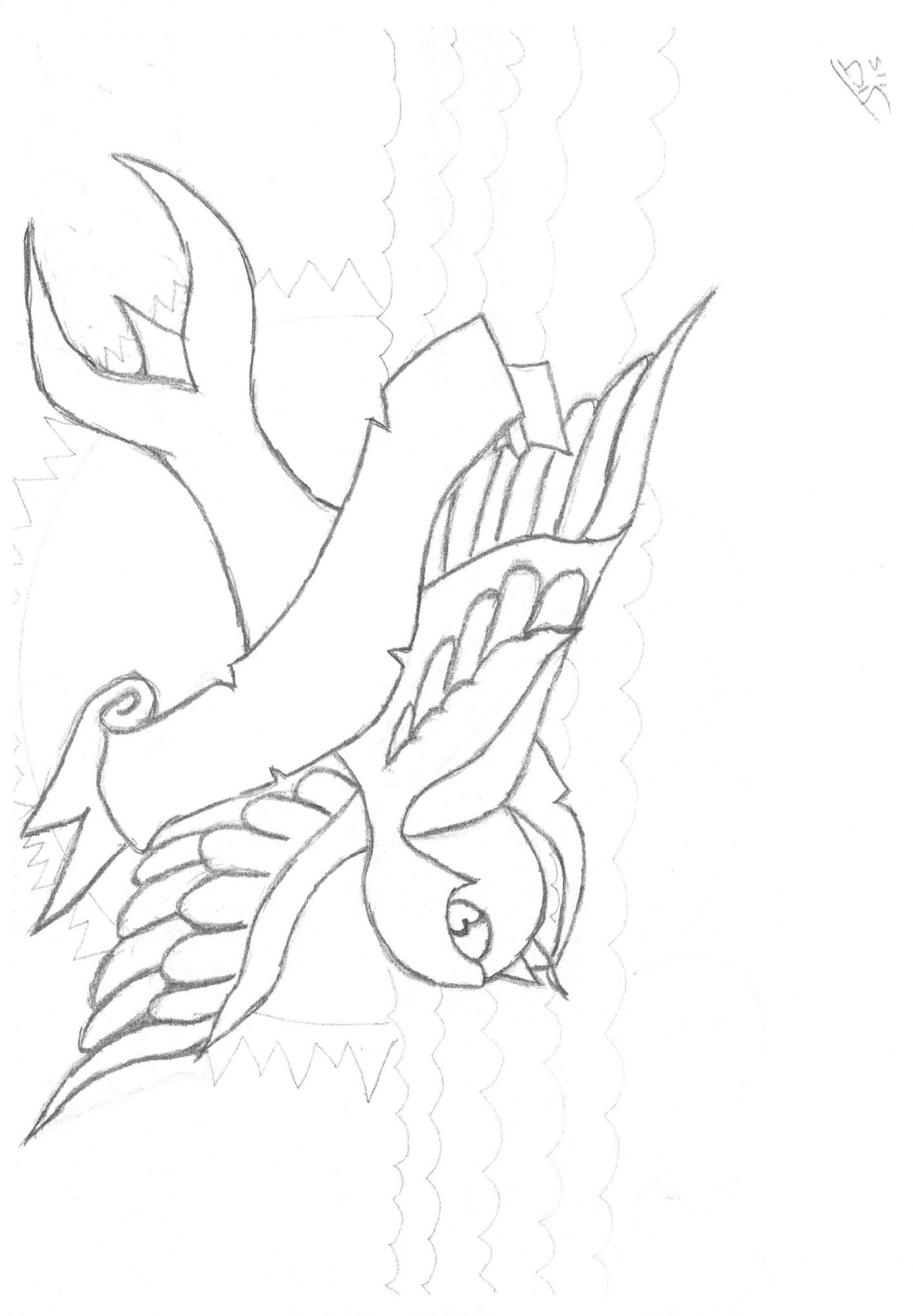

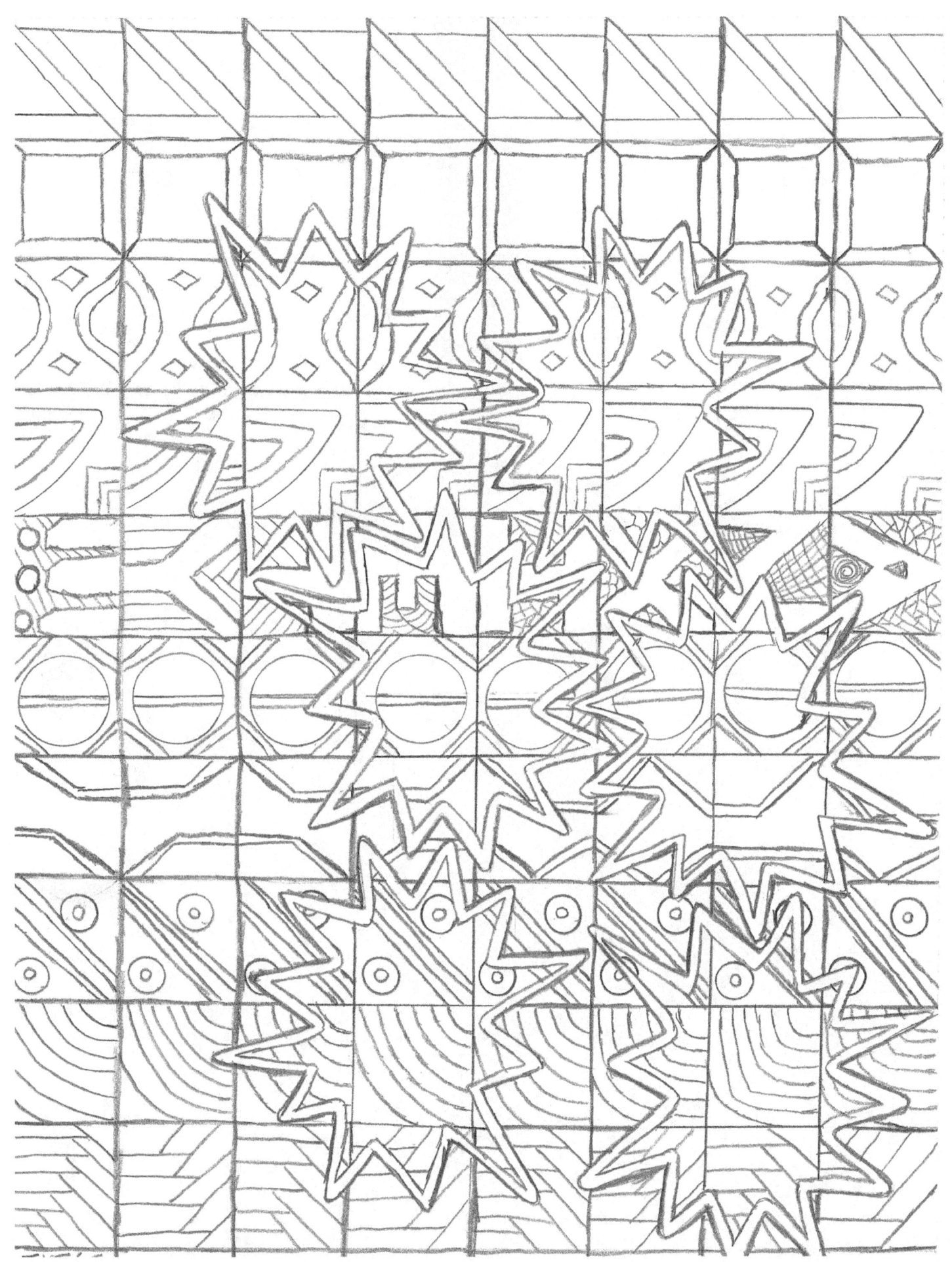

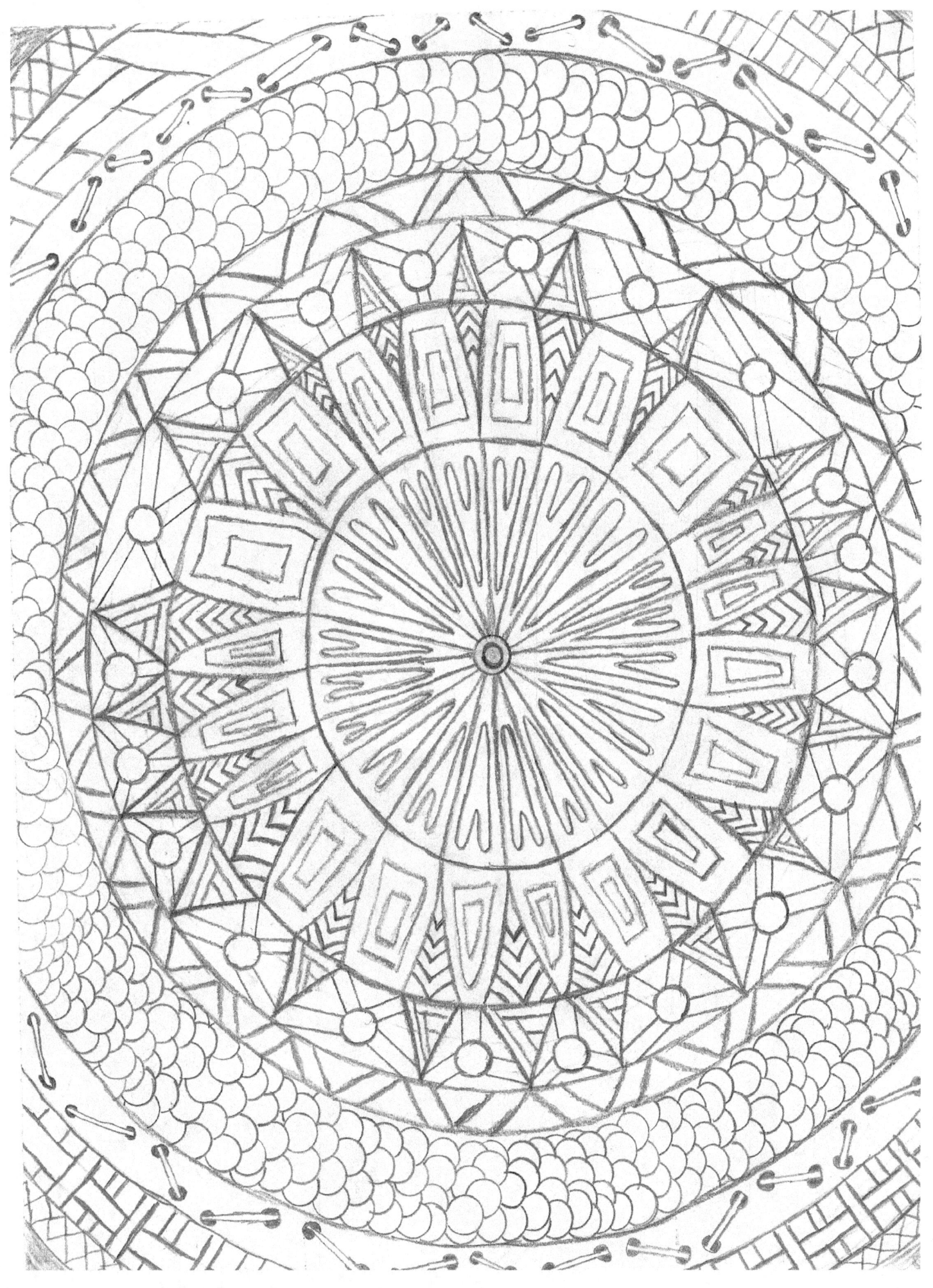

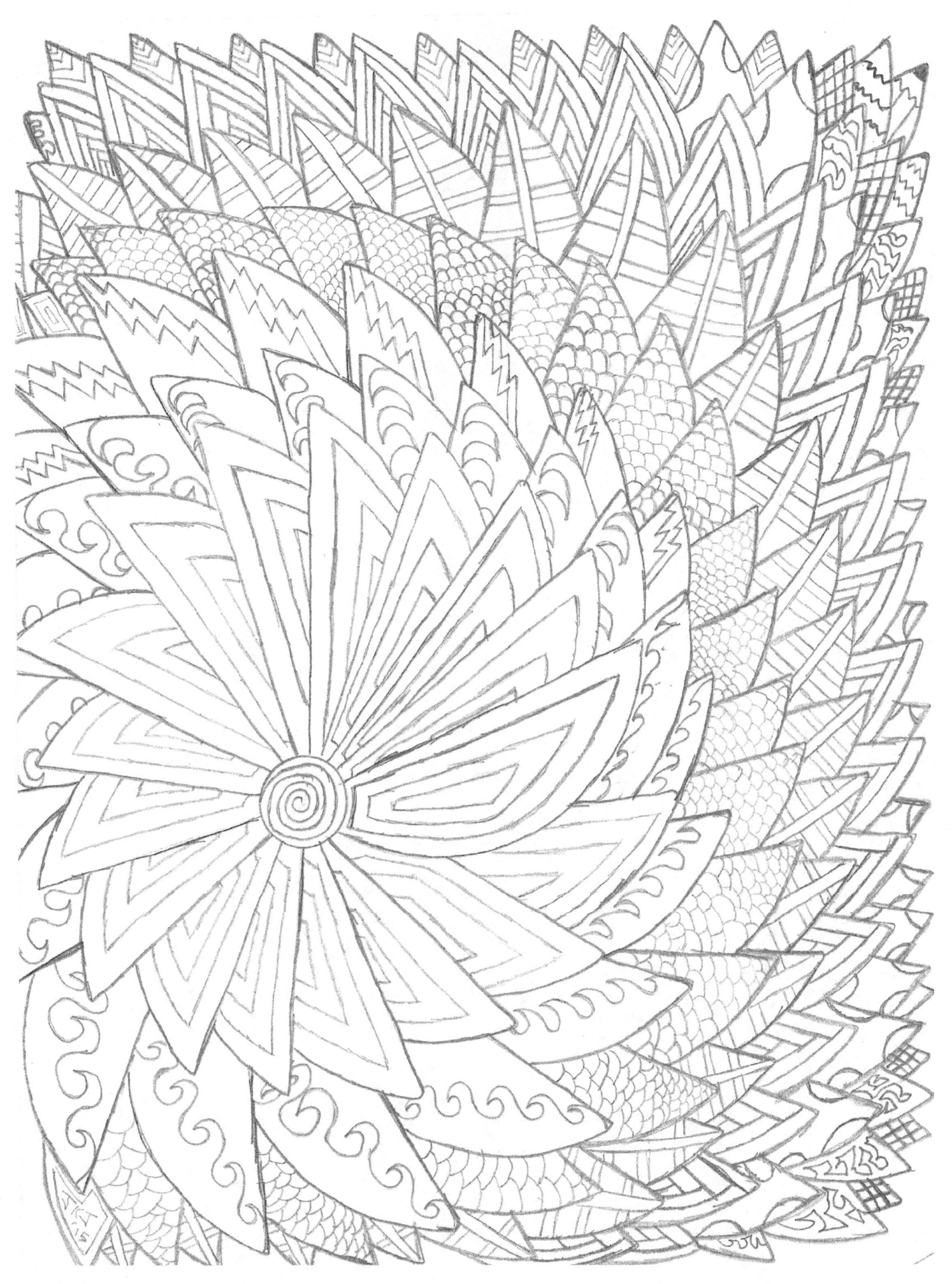

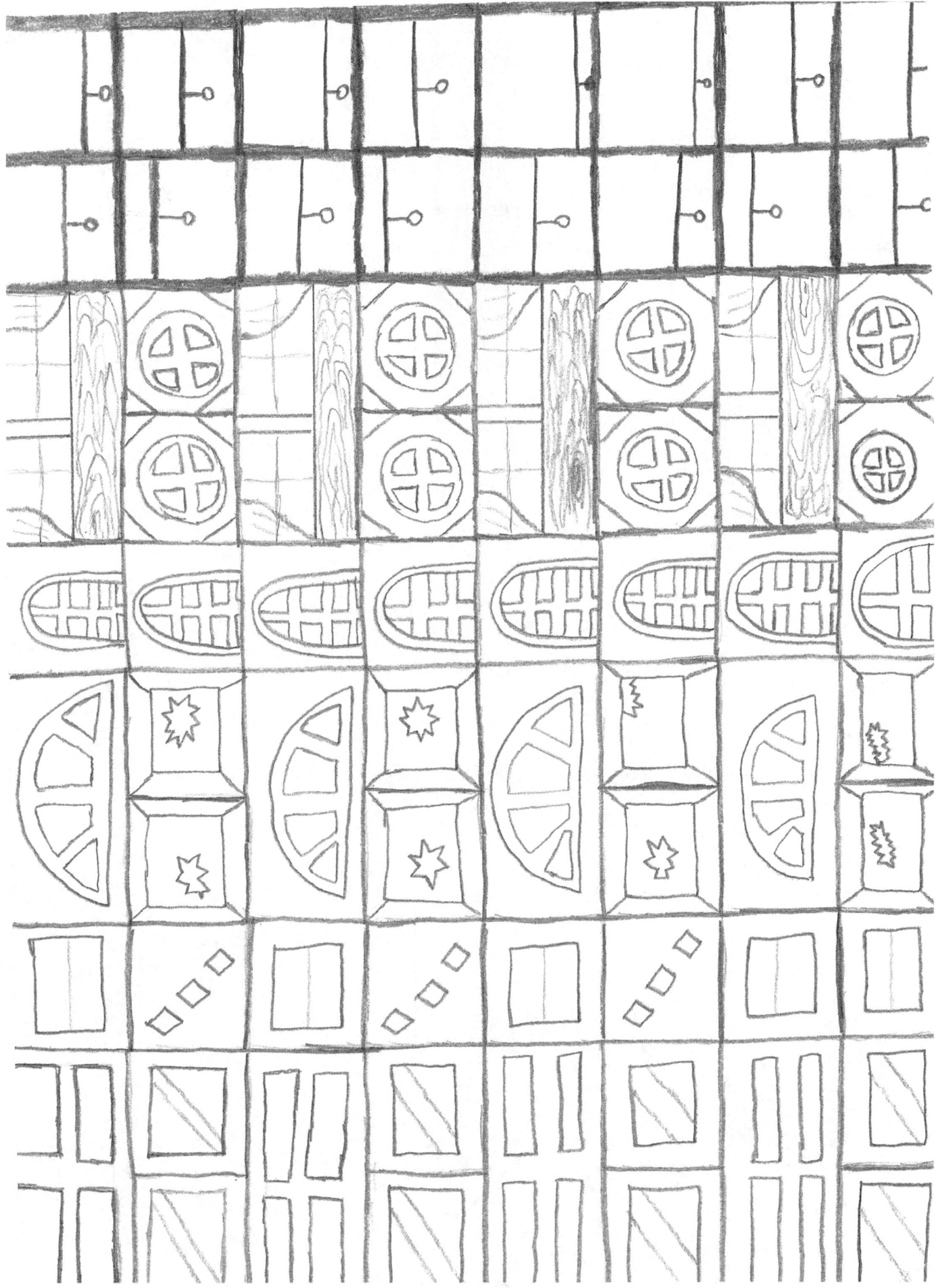

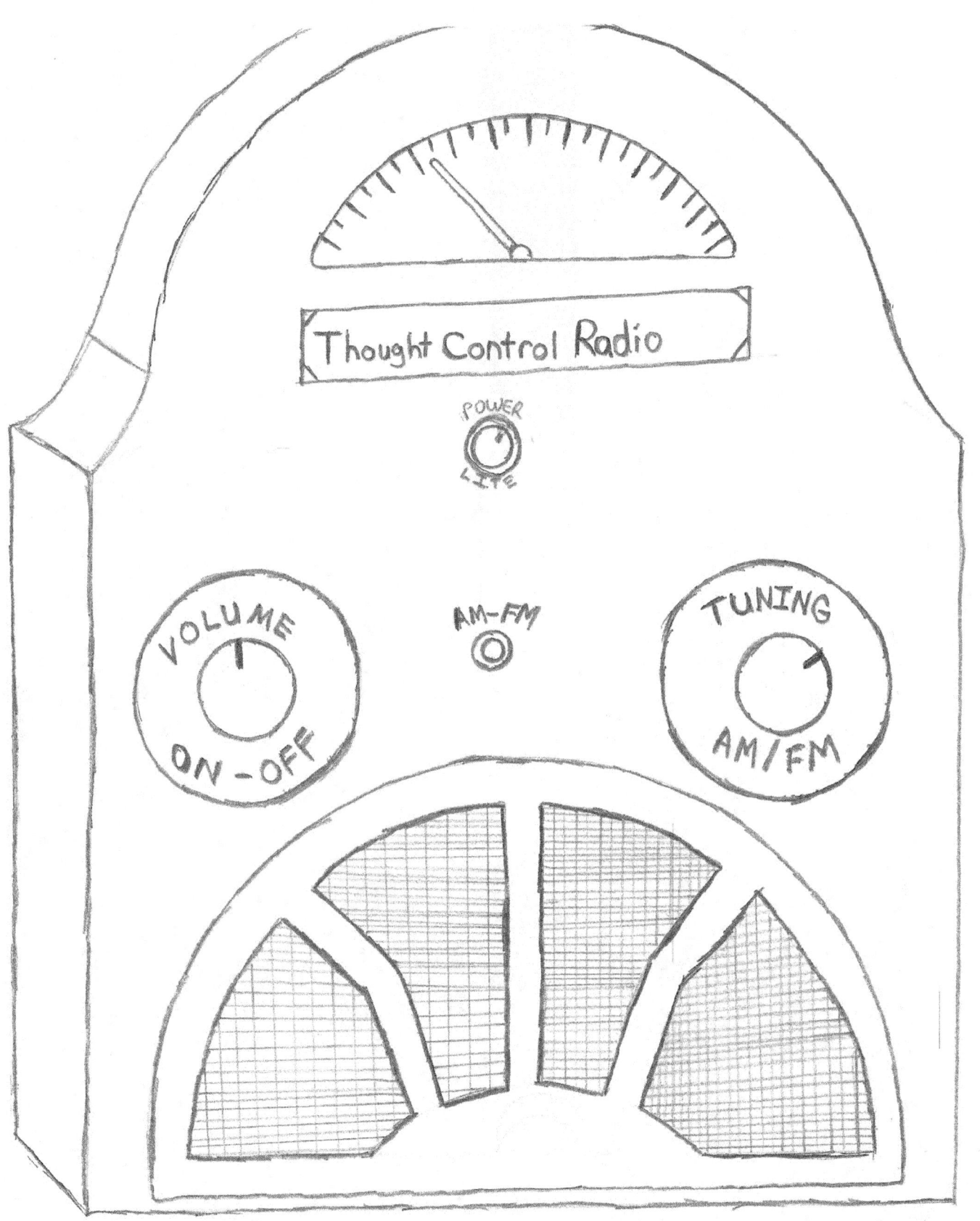

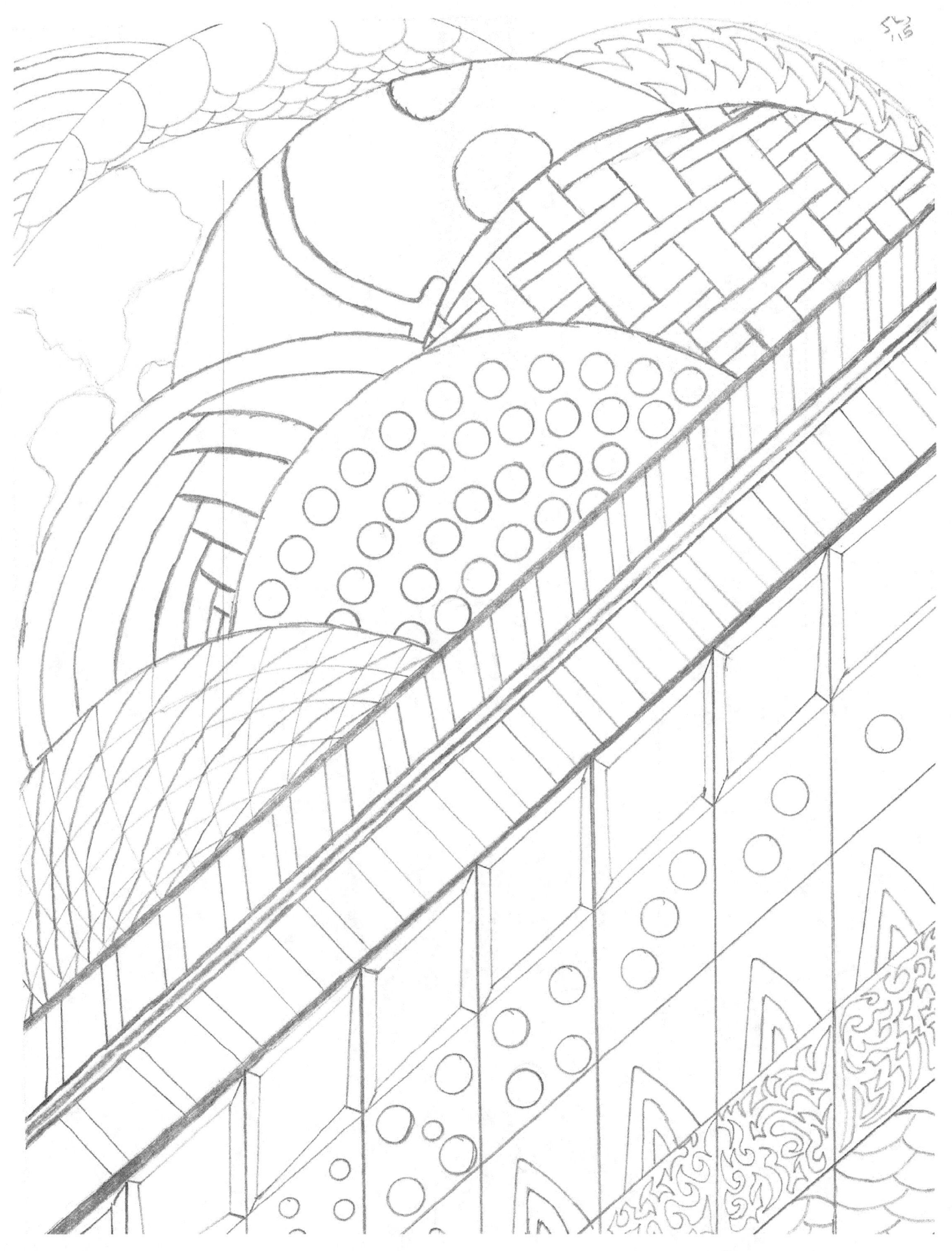

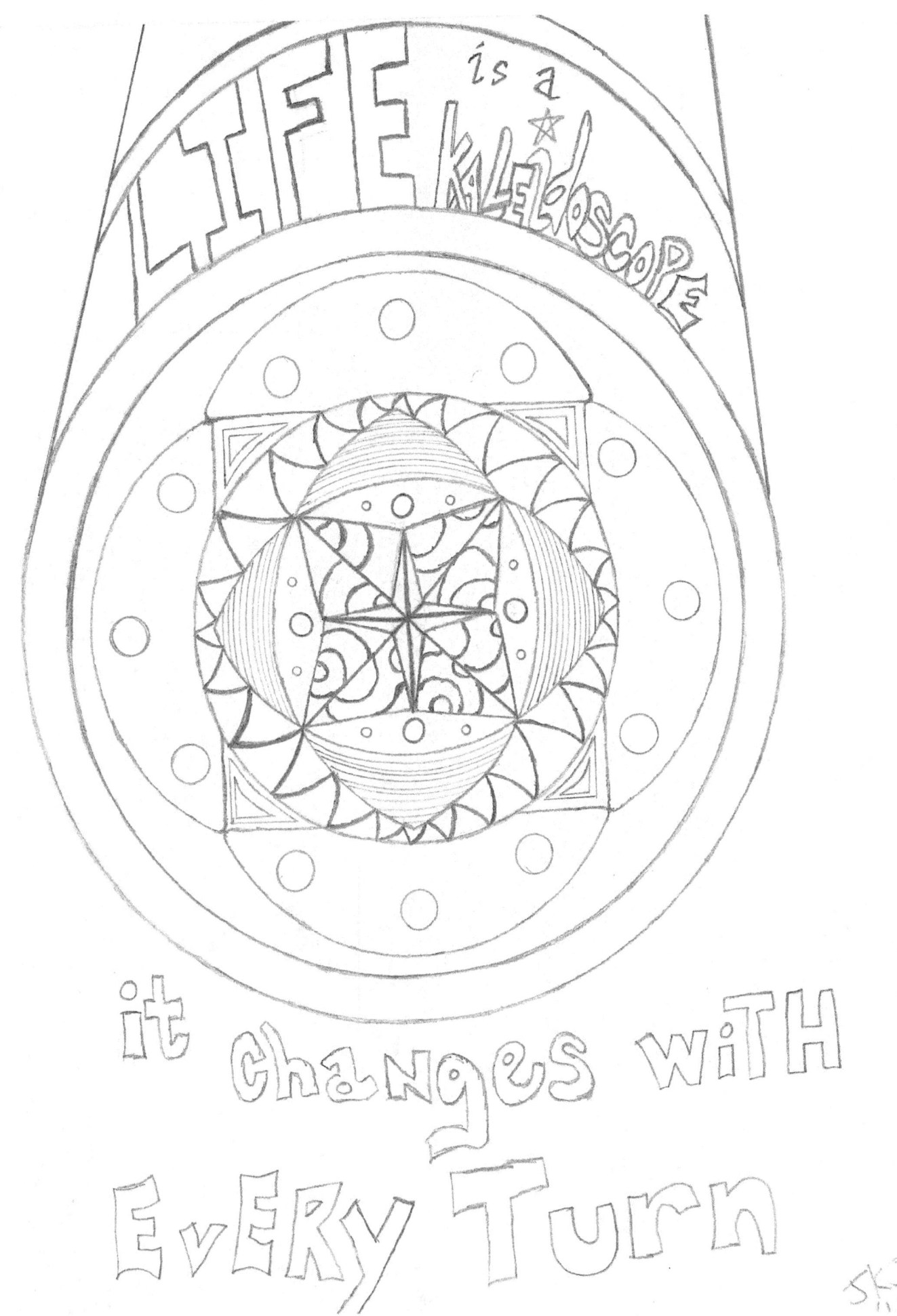

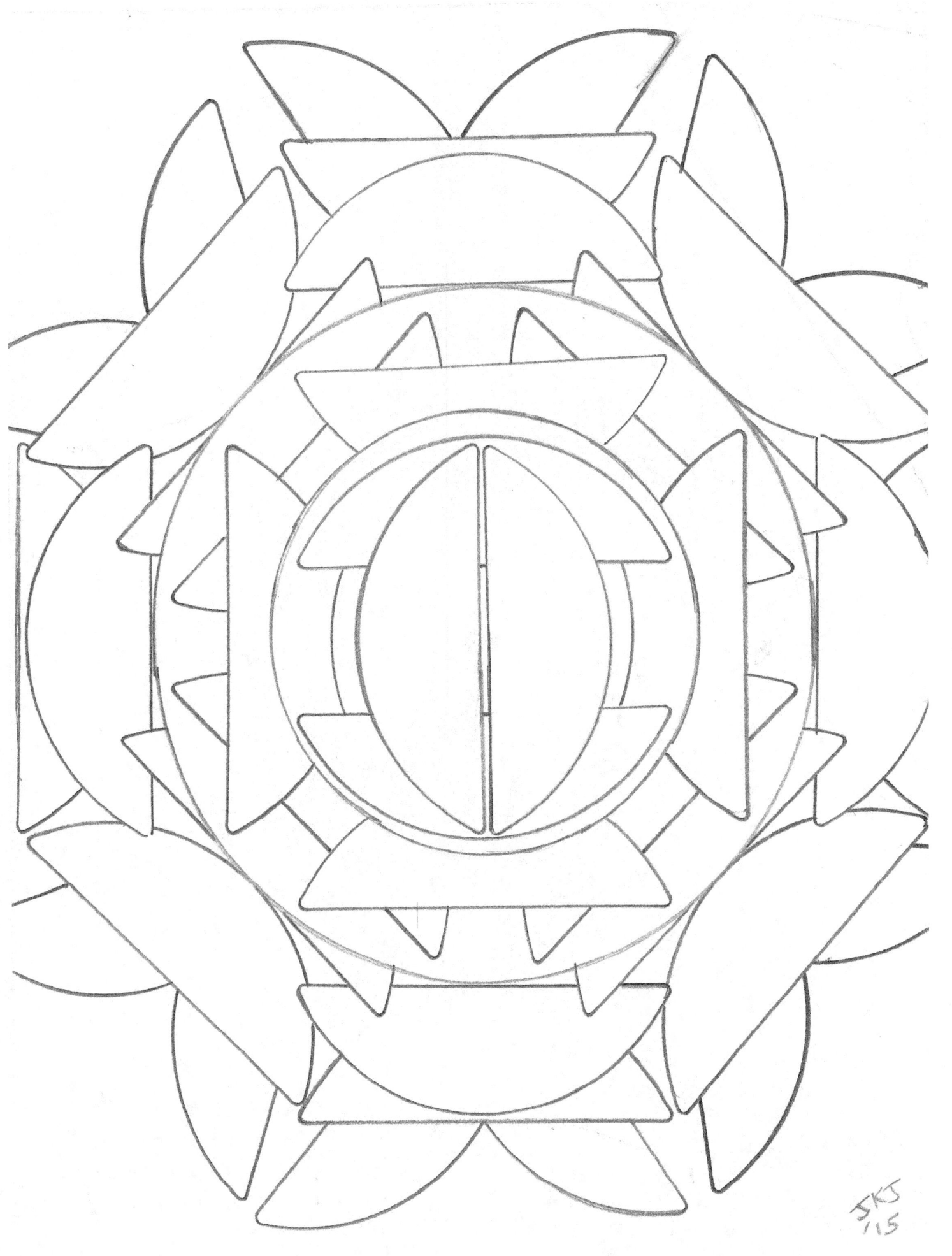

Sometimes WE ARE
THE PIGEON . . .,
Sometimes WE ARE THE
CAR . . .

WHICH DO YOU
CHOOSE TO BE??

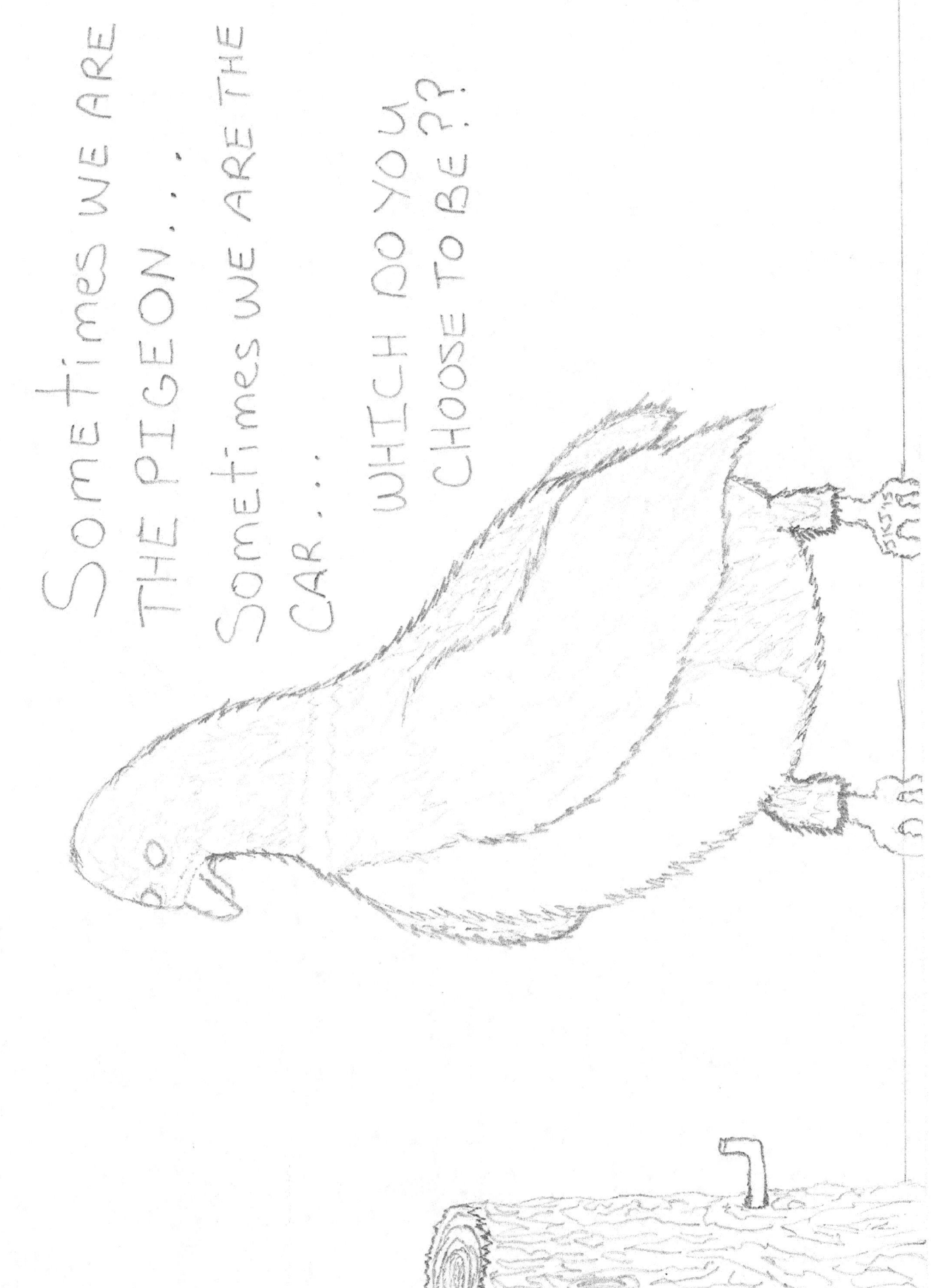

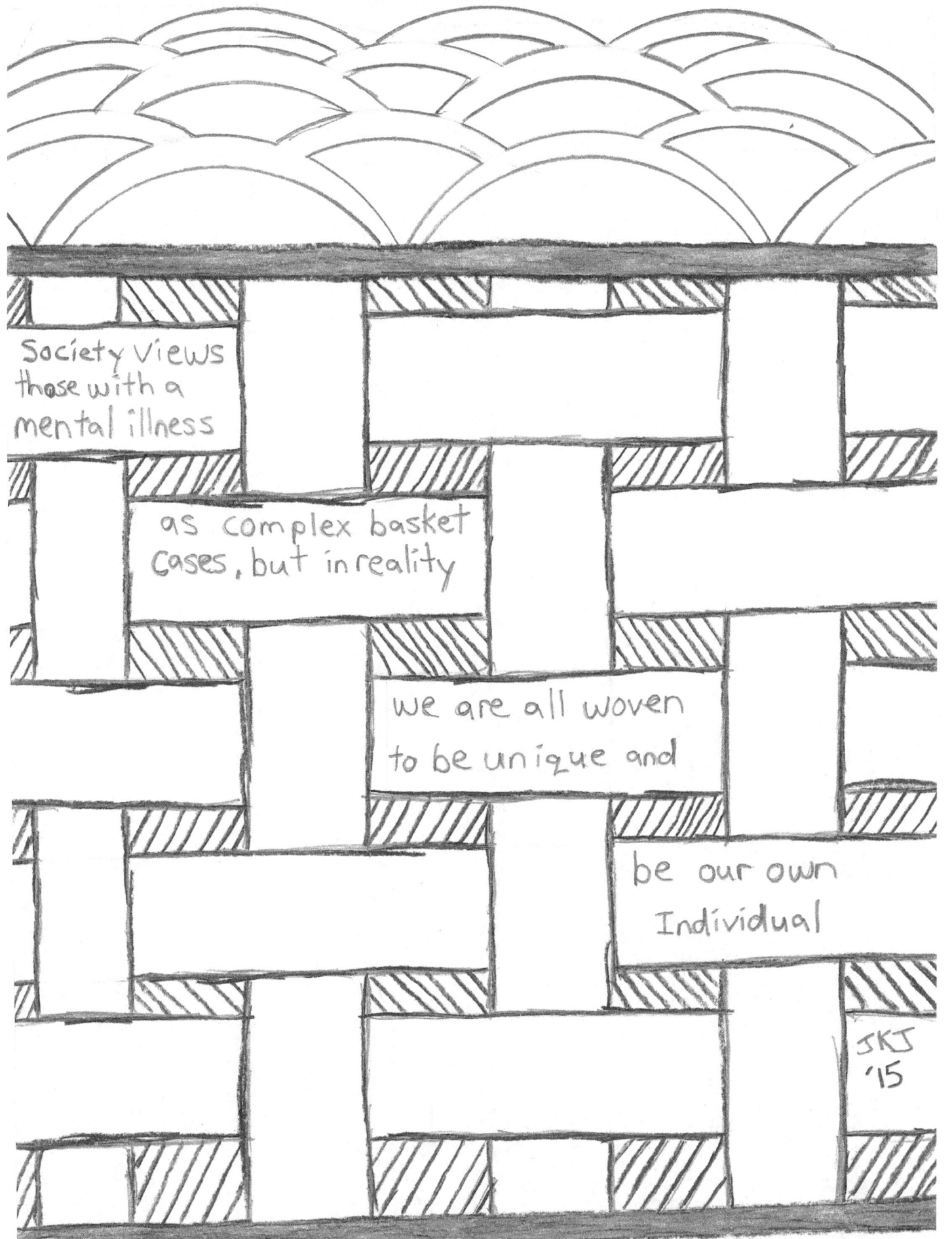

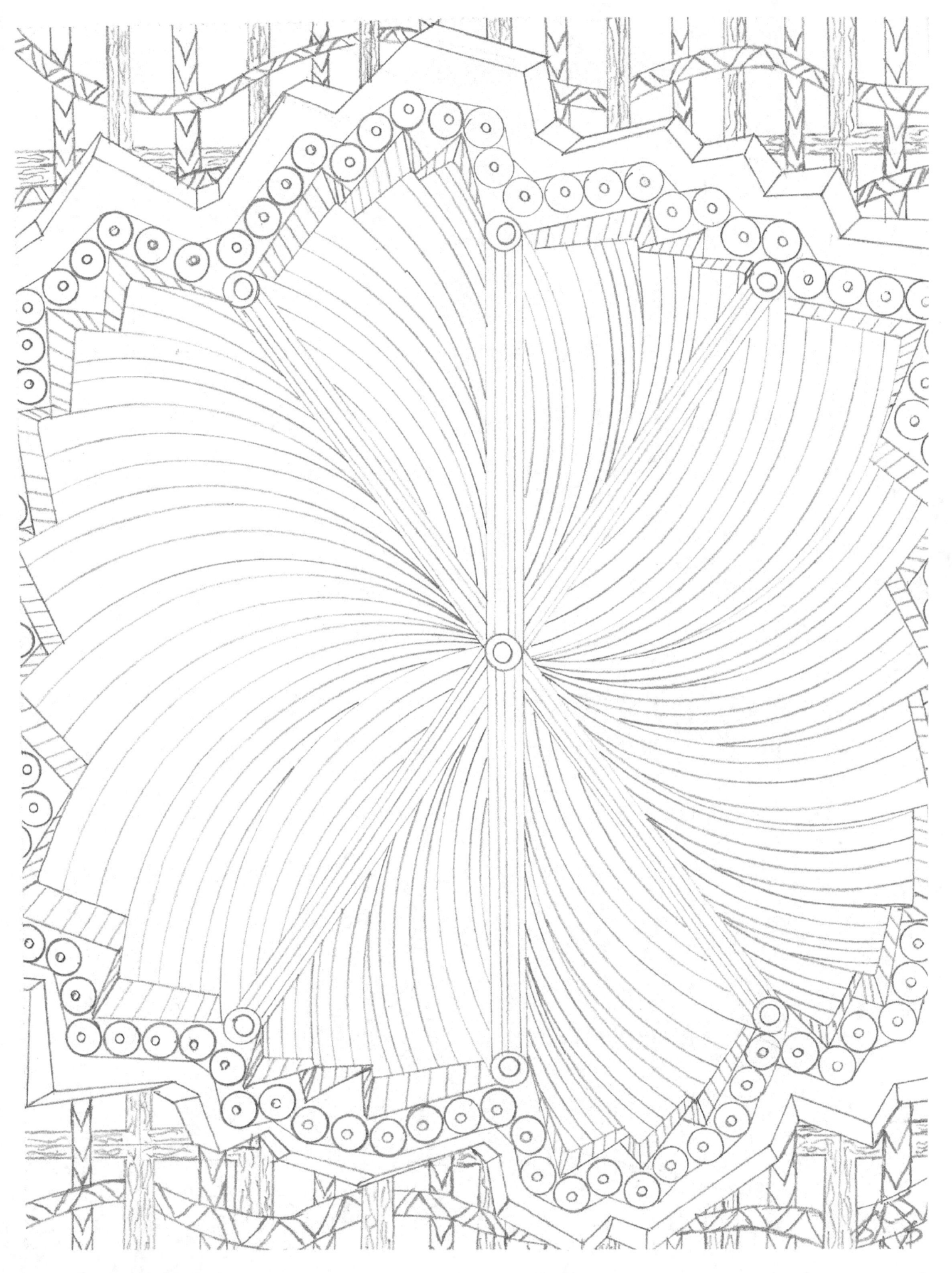

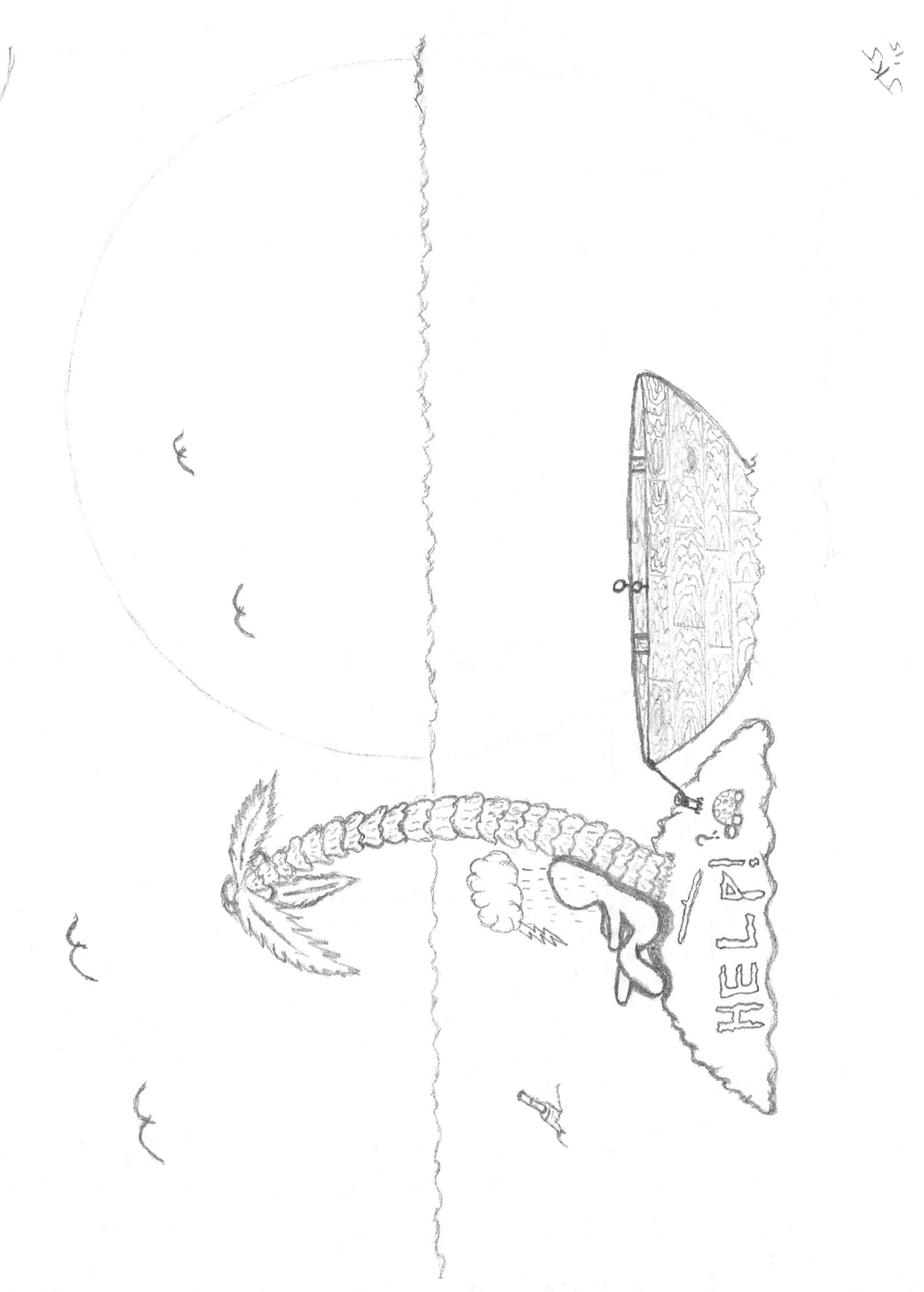

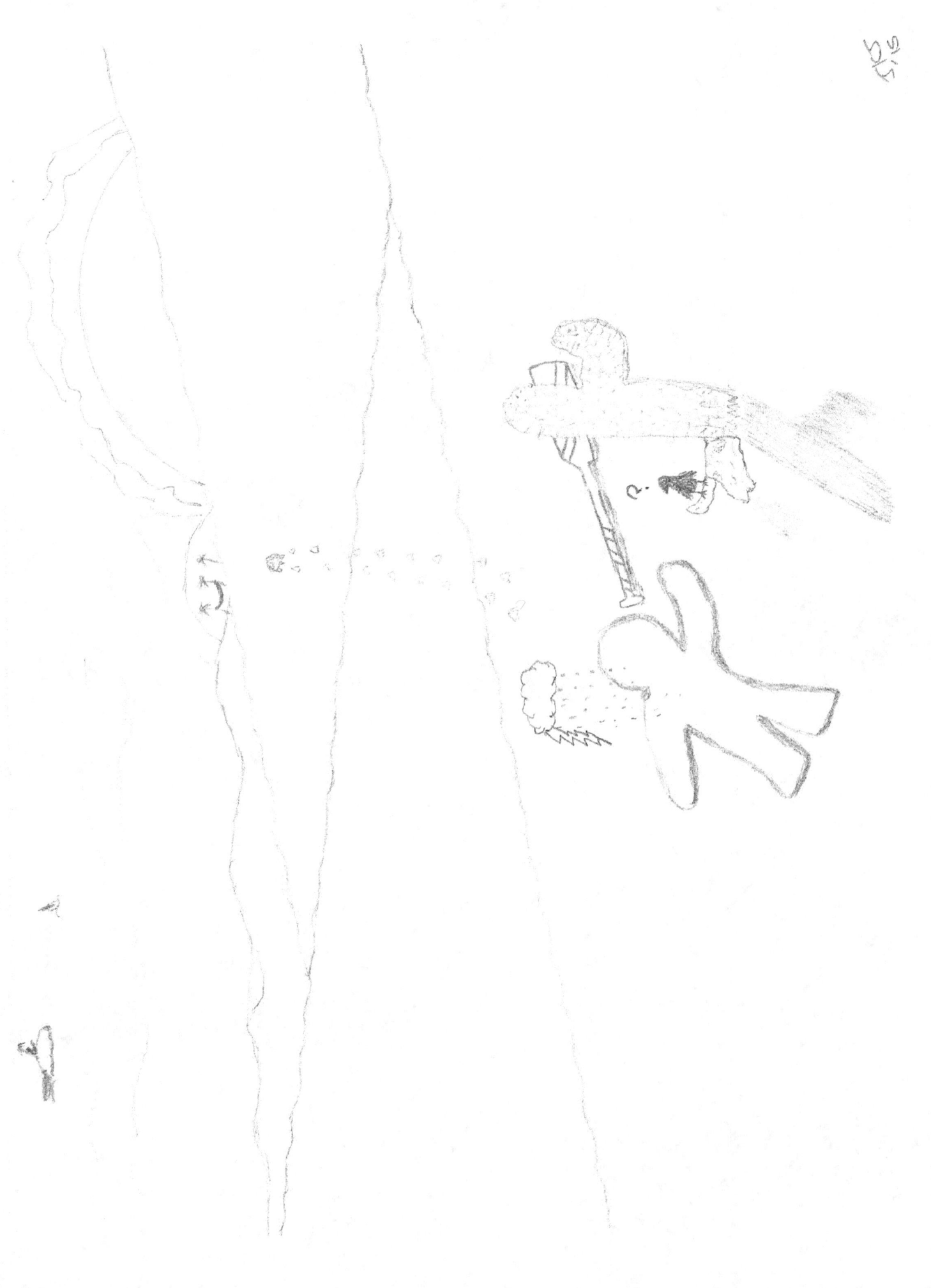

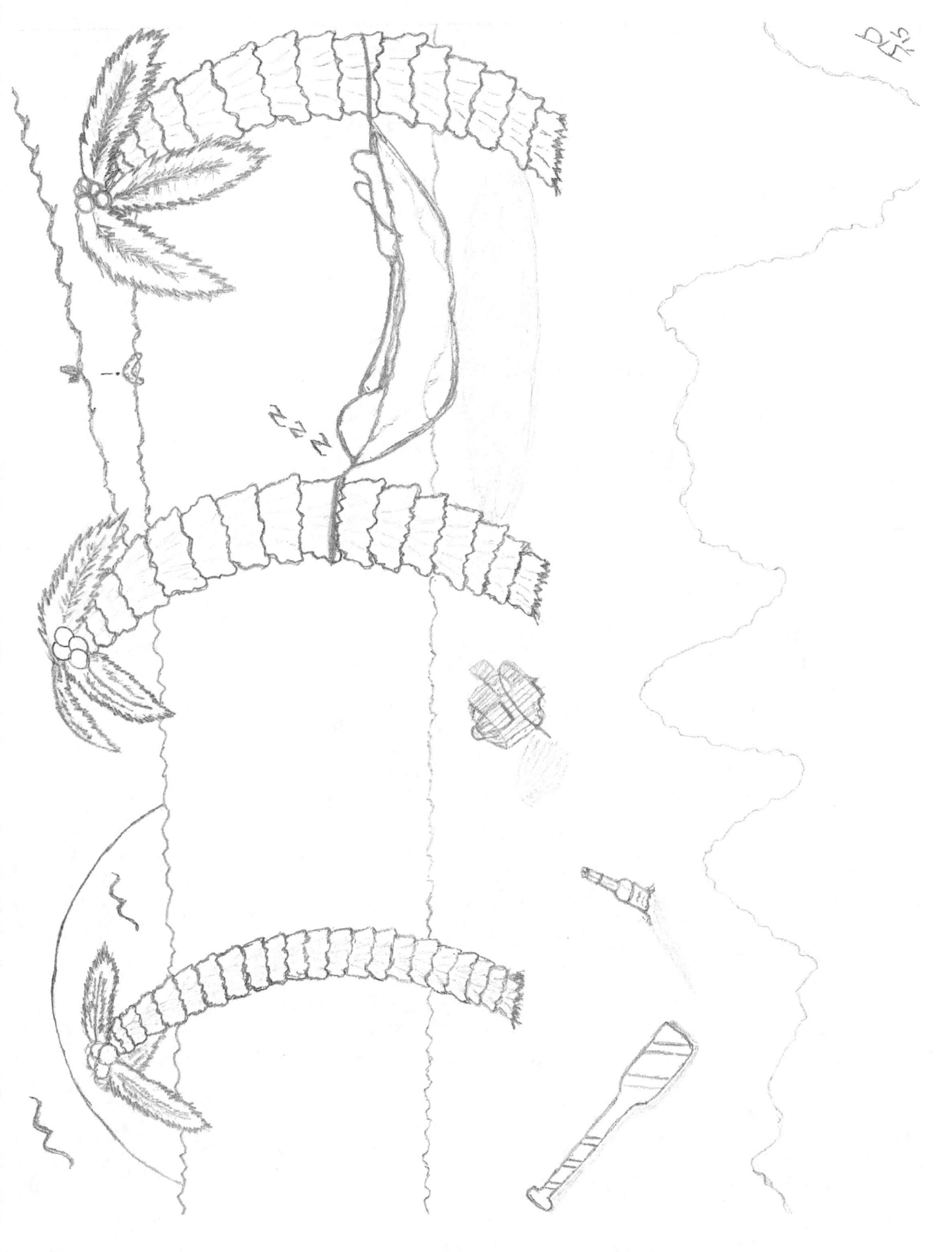

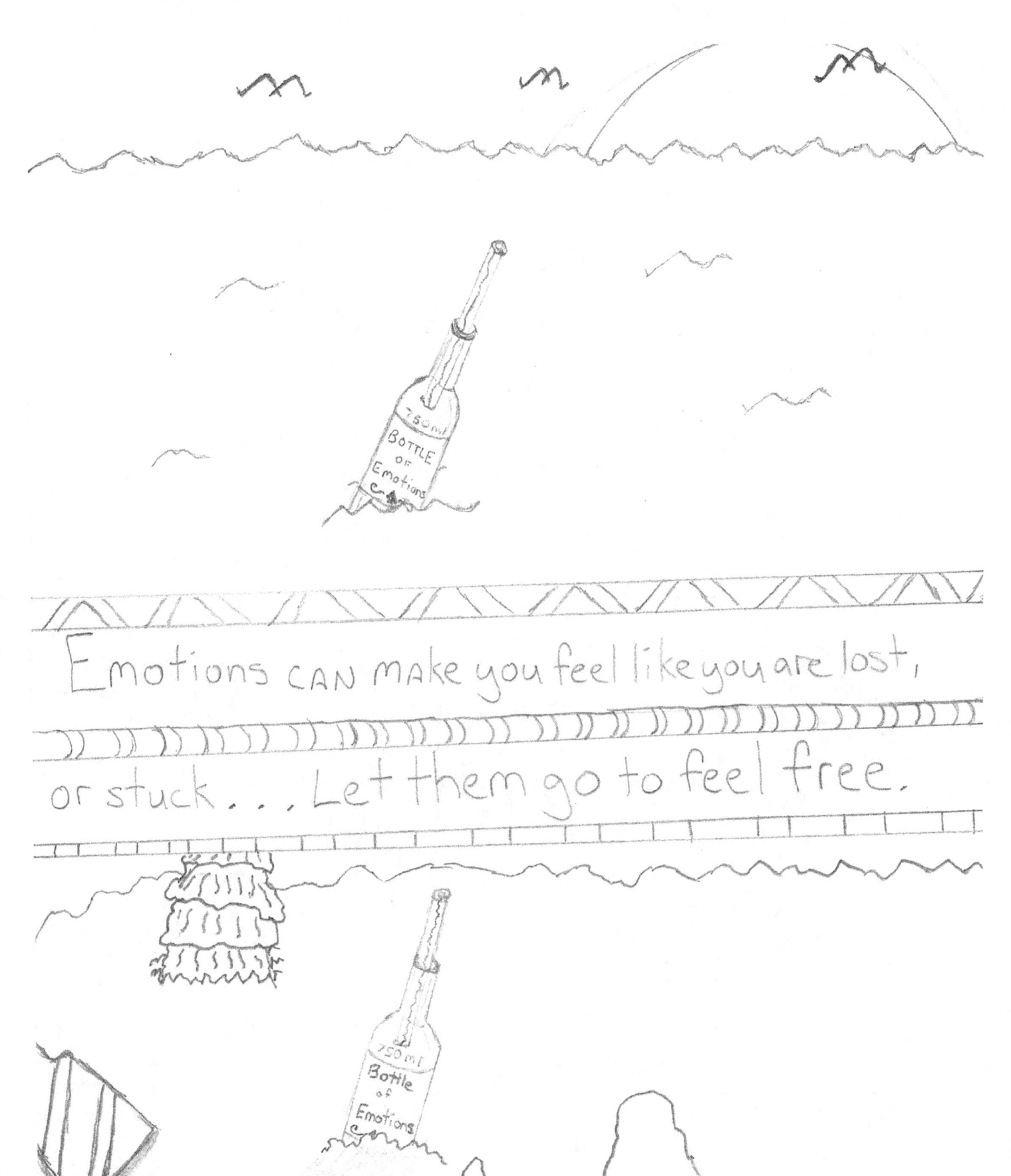

Emotions can make you feel like you are lost, or stuck. . . . Let them go to feel free.

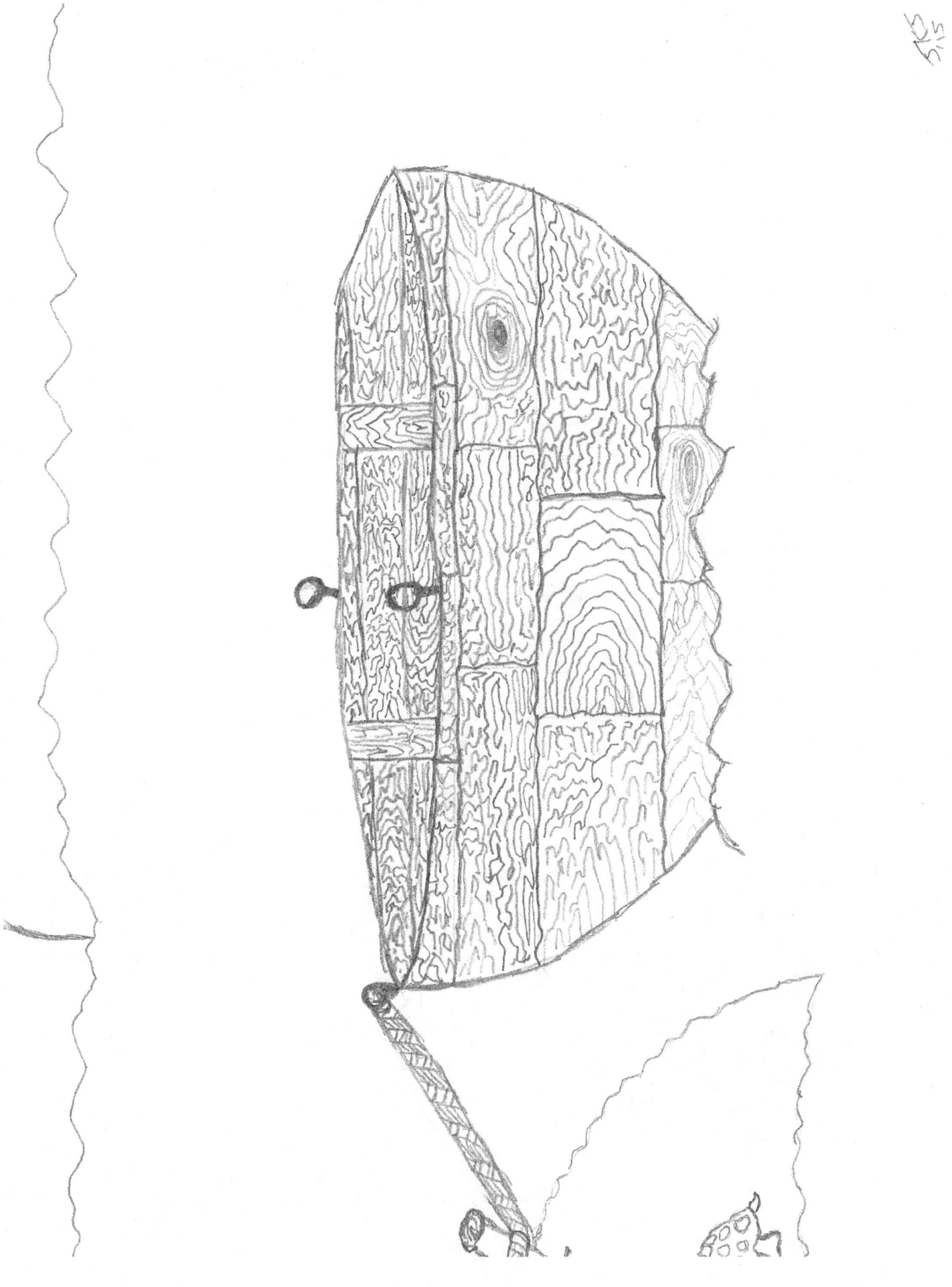

It does not
matter where
you are planted.

What matters
the most is how
you are nutured
and grow within
your enviroment.

Be yourself...
Be Unique.

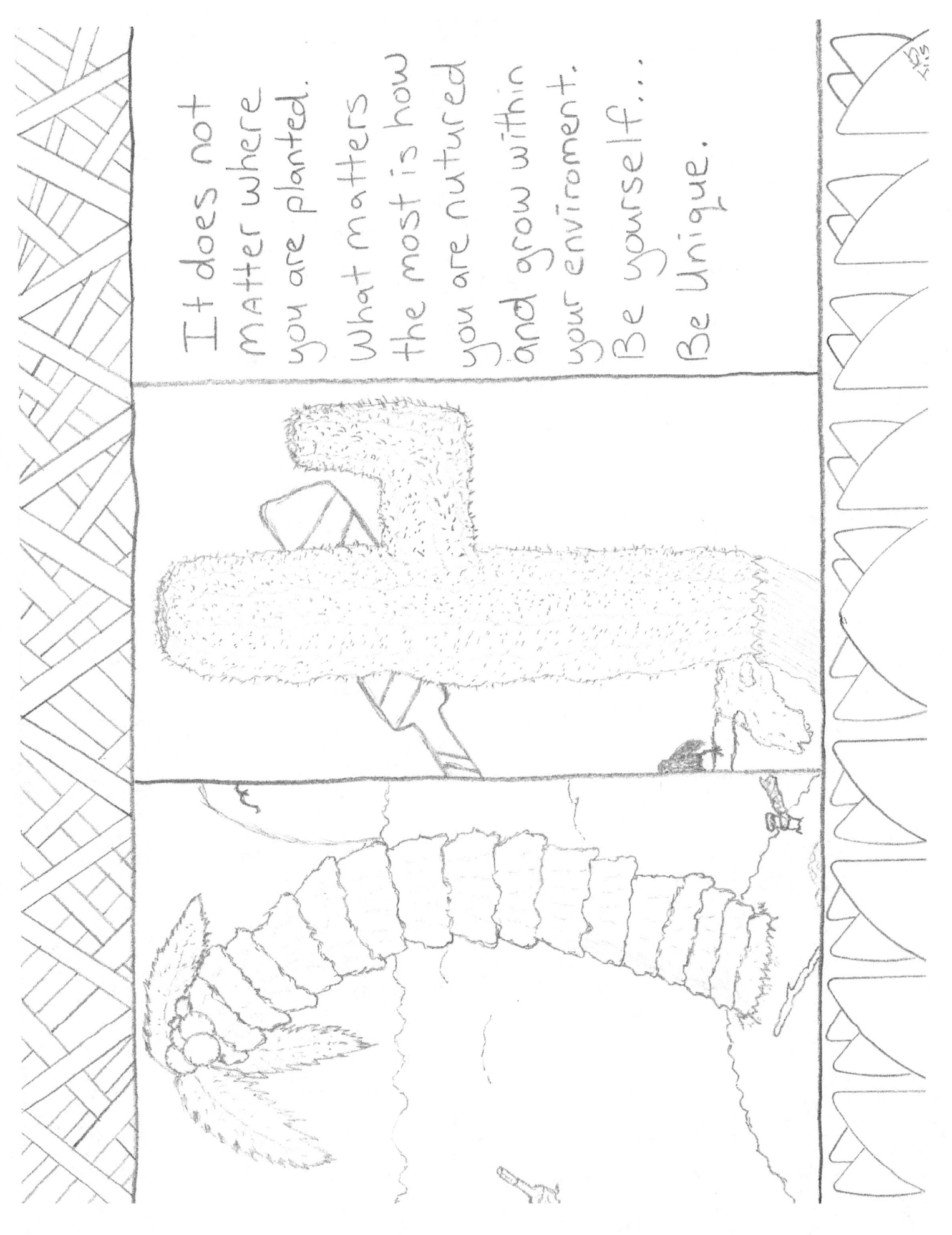

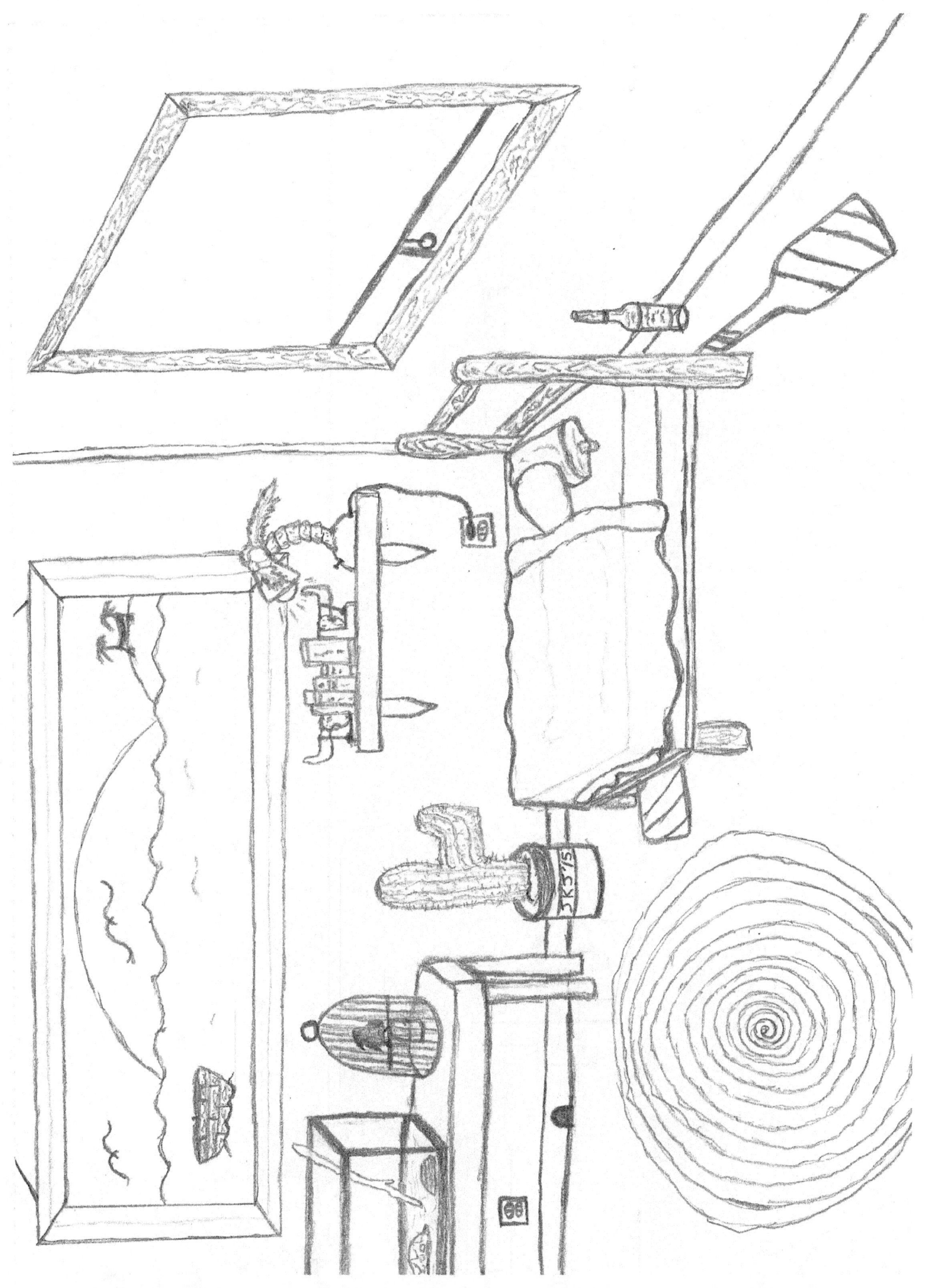

Special Drawing contributed by Emma Jones

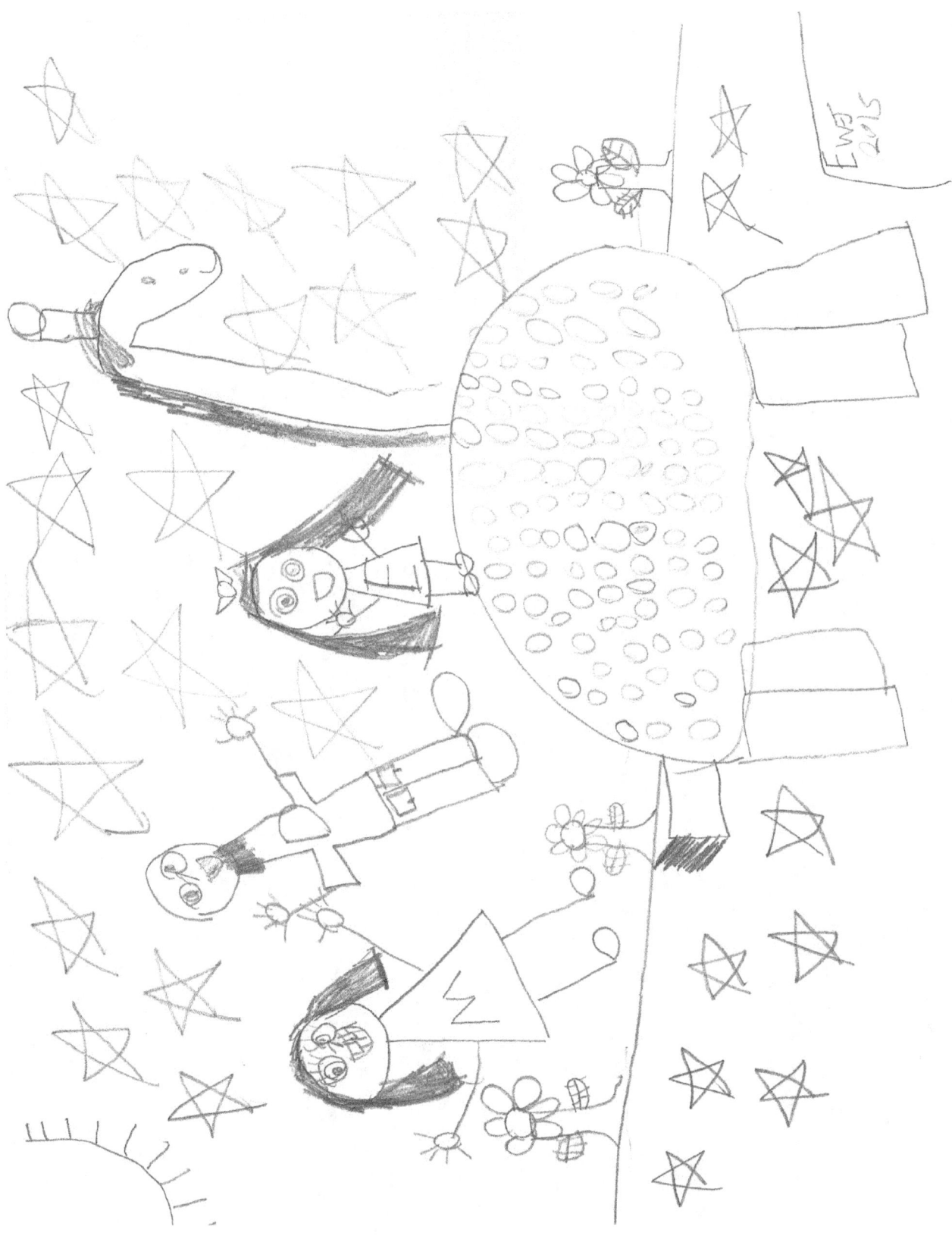